amuse-bouche

photographs by TIM TURNER

 RANDOM HOUSE NEW YORK

amuse-bouche

RICK TRAMONTO

with MARY GOODBODY

little bites that delight
before the meal begins

LIBRARY OF CONGRESS CATALOGING-IN-PUBLICATION DATA

Tramonto, Rick.
Amuse-Bouche : little bites that delight
before the meal begins / Rick Tramonto.
p.   cm.
ISBN 0-375-50760-4 (alk. paper)
1. Appetizers.   I. Title.
TX740.T714   2002
641.8′12—dc21   2002022651

PRINTED IN CHINA ON ACID-FREE PAPER

RANDOM HOUSE WEBSITE ADDRESS: WWW.ATRANDOM.COM

9 8 7 6 5 4 3 2

FIRST EDITION

Book design by Barbara M. Bachman

To my Lord and Savior Jesus Christ, who always leads me down the right road
and who brings me through every storm every time.

To my son, Giorgio Montana Gand Tramonto, who keeps me laughing and
on my toes at all times. I love you.

And to all of my culinary friends and colleagues who were lost
at Windows on the World on September 11, 2001, and their families.
May God bless you; you will never, ever, be forgotten.

acknowledgments

FROM RICK TRAMONTO:

Special thanks to Rich Melman, my mentor, my partner, my friend, my guru. I love you, and thank you for always believing in me.

Thanks to my friend and cowriter, Mary Goodbody, who helped me dish this into words and share with the world the beauty of the *amuse*.

Thanks to my longtime friend and brilliant photographer, Tim Turner, who keeps me focused and challenges me to make every dish the best it can be during those long photo shoots.

Thanks to my supportive and loving family, Eileen Tramonto, Frank Tramonto, Paul and Dorothy Tramonto, Sean and Brian Pschirrer, Ed and Mary Carroll, Gia Tramonto, and Gale Gand, who have shown me how to live and breathe outside the culinary world.

Thanks to my spiritual family, Pastors Gregory and Grace Dickow of Life Changers International Church, for their love and blessings, and for feeding me the word of God. Also to Van and Doni Crouch for Winning 101, and to Pastor Tom Bouvier and Bonnie Bouvier, Pastor Keith Cistrunk, Dr. Creflo Dollar and Taffi Dollar, Bishop T. D. Jakes, Jesse and Cathy Duplantis, and Pastor James McDonald at Walk in the Word for their wisdom and teaching of the word of God.

Thanks to my awesome agent, Jane Dystel, and my editors, Pamela Cannon and Mary Bahr, and the great team at Random House, who always make it seem easy and pleasurable, for their faith in this book and me. Special thanks to Jason Wheeler, my *amuse chef de parti*, for helping me test and organize these recipes in such a cheerful way.

Thanks to my Tru partners, Rich Melman, Gale Gand, Scott Barton, Steve Ottman,

Kevin Brown, Jay Steibre, and Charles Haskel, for their deep friendship and for giving me a stage to play on every day.

Thanks to my magnificent eighty-member staff at Tru, who make it happen every day, for their dedication and loyalty. Especially to my *chef de cuisine*, Mark Andelbradt; my sous-chefs, Jason Robinson, Mark Bernal, Brad Parsons, and Elliot Bowles; my great management team; and my sommelier (the "wine guy"), Scott Tyree.

I would also like to thank the city of Chicago, Mayor Richard M. Daley, and the food press for supporting me and allowing me to hone my craft in this great city. A very special thanks to my vendors and the farmers across the country who work so hard to find and grow the best-of-the-best ingredients and products for me to use.

Thanks to those who inspire me on a daily basis and who support my culinary efforts: Oprah Winfrey, Pierre Gagnaire, Emeril Lagasse, Julia Child, José Andrés, Ferran and Albert Adria, Jean-Georges Vongerichten, Alain Ducasse, Bobby Flay, Alfred Portale, Mario Batali, Patrick O'Connell, Nobu Matsuhisa, Martha Stewart, Guy Savoy, Juan Mari and Elana Arzak, David Bouley, Danny Wegman, Randy Zeiban, Gray Kunz, Norman Van Aken, Charlie Trotter, Thomas Keller, Martin Berasategui, Michael Lamonaco, Daniel Boulud, Michael Chiarello, Wolfgang Puck, Francois Payard, Greg Bromen, Jean-Louis Palladin, Alan Wong, Rick Bayless, Tom Colicchio, and Roger Verge.

Thanks to my supportive friends whom I rarely get to see because I'm always working all the time—I love you guys: Thea Gattone for your prayers for this book, Larry and Julie Binstein, Vinnie and Theresa Rupert, the late Bob Payton and Wendy Payton, Muhammad Salahuddin, Angela and Veronica Petrucci, Debra Ferrer and Jim Visger, Joan Cusack, Harold and Erica Ramis, Al Lipkin, Ina Pinkney (the breakfast queen), John Coletta, Jimmy Bonnesteel, Val Landsburg, Marty Tiersky, Rochelle and Gary Fleck (thanks for all the great Chefwear), and all of the folks at Lettuce Entertain You. You're the best.

FROM MARY GOODBODY:

Heartfelt thanks to Rick Tramonto for welcoming me so enthusiastically to this project, for his generosity of spirit, patience, knowledge, and good humor, which kept the telephone lines humming and e-mails flying. I also want to thank our agent, Jane Dystel, for gently but firmly guiding the project from proposal to final book; our Random House editors, Pamela Cannon and Mary Bahr, for their belief in the book and their hard work; Carole Harlam for her careful help with recipe editing; and Laura Goodbody, who cheerfully pitched in to help where needed during the final, hectic weeks and who always supports and believes in her mom.

contents

introduction

AMUSE:
To entertain or occupy in a light, playful, or pleasant manner;
to appeal to the sense of humor; to supply amusement or diversion
by specially prepared or contrived methods.

AMUSE-BOUCHE:

Little bites of food to amuse the mouth,
invigorate the palate, whet the appetite.

I vividly recall my first trip to France in 1980. After the plane landed, I waited impatiently in line at immigration. As soon as I left the terminal, I grabbed a cab and raced into Paris, worried that I might miss my reservation at Jamin, Joël Robuchon's famed restaurant. I had booked the table at least six months earlier, and during my flight across the Atlantic, my taste buds were primed for the meal to come. Once I was seated in the beautiful, flower-filled room, a tiny bite of ethereal food was placed in front of me. It was my very first exposure to the custom of greeting a diner with *amuse-bouche*.

I was completely charmed, and immediately made *amuse-bouche* part of my own menus. Over the years, I have become well known for them, which is a reputation I am happy to have. I especially appreciate the high level of hospitality that an *amuse* conveys, because for me, hospitality is the bedrock of a great restaurant.

Everyone who walks into my restaurant, Tru, is greeted with an *amuse-bouche*— an intriguing bite of absolutely delicious food that is my way of saying, "Welcome, I hope you enjoy your meal." Other fine restaurants practice this very French tradition, but I have a true passion for it. These little treats are so tasty, so exquisitely rendered, so beautifully presented and jewellike, that today I offer eight selections. We recently served four customers at a single table twelve *amuse* each, an event that turned their evening into a kind of sit-down cocktail party. This led to the creation of our *amuse* tasting menu.

At Tru, we are so well known for our *amuse*, that we prepare more than five hundred pieces of six to eight different ones every day. The selection changes constantly, depending on the season, the availability of ingredients, and, I freely admit, how whimsical I am feeling. All of the offerings receive the same attention to detail and fine ingredients that you will find in the recipes on these pages.

Until now, no book has focused on these tiny culinary treasures. There have been books about hors d'oeuvres, tapas, and appetizers. Made a little larger, many of my *amuse-bouche* are lovely when served in these ways. I do hope, though, that you will kick off your next dinner party or holiday feast with an *amuse* or two, and delight in the enchantment they will bring to your table.

THE FUN OF THE AMUSE

I love the *amuse* because it allows me to both create dishes that are absolutely perfect and beautiful and to have a zany sense of fun. At Tru, we like to call our cuisine "fine dining with a sense of humor." The *amuse* appeals to my philosophy that no one should take food too seriously, even while they are serious about food. I cook as a way to express love, nurturing, and comfort. I don't approach it intellectually, although I admire those who do. To me, food should, above all else, taste good. If it does not, you run the risk of cooking soulless food. What could be sadder?

I am not formally trained, although I have apprenticed my craft with some of the best chefs in the business and have learned in some of the finest kitchens. Because of this, I have come to appreciate the spectrum of what is the best—be it the best burger or the best foie gras, the best French fries or the best caviar. My culinary education has been a movable feast, a school without walls. This encourages me to think outside the box. I may be grounded in proper technique but I am not tethered to it, which explains why I so love the *amuse*.

None of the *amuse* recipes is particularly complicated, although many rely on ingredients you might not use every day. I cherish cooking with all that the good green earth has to offer, often straying from the known to create little gems with foods with which I may not be as familiar. But, let's face it, at the end of the day, beyond tasting good, food's mission is to bring joy, excitement, and pleasure to the heart, soul, and all five senses. I hope these recipes inspire you—I do not mean for them to intimidate in any way. These recipes are simple, delicious, and accessible. Have fun!

THE BEST INGREDIENTS

An *amuse* is meant to tickle the palate, to bewitch the eye and tongue, but because it is not the main course or even the first course, it can also be lighthearted and provocative. The concept may be new to you, but once you grasp it, let your imagination run wild. Add your own creative twists and turns, and use this tiny first course to indulge in exotic or expensive ingredients, to try new cooking techniques, or to use those plates and cups that don't quite fit with the rest of your dinnerware.

An *amuse* should explode in the mouth with flavor and texture. After meeting this criterion, it can be elegant or casual, made with expensive or everyday ingredients. For example, the Forest Mushroom Terrine (page 42) is a great way to try the cream-, beige-, and mahogany-colored mushrooms overflowing in greenmarket baskets every fall. On a more humble level, if you've never cooked grits, try the Creamy Corn Grits with Butternut Squash and Sweet Corn (page 72) and discover their wonderful versatility and kinship with polenta.

Both the Red, Gold, White, and Candy-Striped Beets with Beet Juice Reduction (page 36) and the Heirloom Tomatoes, "Panzanella Style" (page 32) exemplify how I exalt in exploiting the seasons. When beets or tomatoes are at their best, I buy every variety I can lay my hands on for the sheer joy of experiencing their colors, textures, and subtle differences in taste.

Nothing beats a carefully tended fruit or vegetable at its peak, and this explains why I organized the recipes according to season. As do many chefs and farmers, I feel passionate about respecting the seasons. How else can we avoid depleting the planet and guarantee that there is abundant and pure food for our children and grandchildren? It's no hardship to wait for spring for plump, juicy strawberries or fall for crisp apples. The anticipation only serves to make the experience that much more enjoyable. I wait all year for perfectly ripe watermelon so I can serve Watermelon Cube with Aged Balsamic Vinegar (page 34). No dish is purer than this one and no recipe underscores better how the best ingredients conspire to create the most pristine and best-tasting food.

EXPERIMENT WITH LUXURY

If many of these recipes allow the home cook to experiment with fresh, simple flavors and seasonal foods, others are opportunities to luxuriate in ingredients that may be too expensive, too intense, or too foreign to serve on a large scale. Ocean-fresh squid, sweet-tasting lobster, inky imported caviar, voluptuous foie gras, heady truffles, sumptuous sweetbreads, tiny quail eggs, aged balsamic vinegar, and delicate zucchini blossoms qualify as foods many home cooks would love to serve but are not sure how to do so. The same is true for crumbly imported cheeses, sushi-quality tuna, Norwegian salmon, rich smoked goose breast, fruity extra-virgin olive oil, and juicy, deep-red blood oranges.

This, then, is the glory of the *amuse*. It can be made with nearly anything that catches your fancy. For the curious cook, this is thrilling because it means that the small bottle of rich nut oil, the seductive fat-streaked Italian Parma ham, the plump, briny oysters, the fresh sardines, and the passion fruit puree can find a place at the dinner party, regardless of what is planned for later. An *amuse* does not necessarily have bearing on the rest of the meal.

This is reassuring, but so is the reality that many of these *amuse* can become significant players. For instance, the Chilled Asparagus Soup with Crème Fraîche (page 4) offers an intense sip of liquid asparagus when served as an *amuse*, yet the recipe can be doubled and served as a first course or very light main course; ditto for the Bulgur Salad with Watercress and Toasted Walnut Puree (page 63). The Asian Soba Noodle Fork with Water Chestnuts (page 172) could be a substantial first course, and the Ahi Tuna Cube with Toasted Black and White Sesame Seeds (page 108) makes an outstanding passed hors d'oeuvre.

This is true of many of the *amuse*. I feel that if an *amuse* is more than a bite and a half, it ceases being an *amuse* and becomes an appetizer. When it's only a bite, it can be an hors d'oeuvre, so elusive is the line between *amuse* and hors d'oeuvre. Hostesses and caterers who complain that they have run out of good ideas for party food need look no further!

TECHNIQUES AND STYLE

For anyone interested in learning new cooking techniques, these recipes are a feast of ideas. Foams seem to be the rage in restaurants coast to coast—and I have an entire chapter devoted to them. I tell you how to make savory sorbets, which are lovely *amuse* as well as palate cleansers and accompaniments for fruit and cheese. I use paper-thin potato slices to wrap fish, make vinaigrettes and infuse oils with truffles, dry summer's tomatoes in the oven, and rely on sheets of gelatin to make the new, lighter aspics so popular now. I garnish these little dishes with pretty greens, fresh herbs, edible flowers, sliced citrus fruit, and glistening caviar. Again, let your own creativity be your guide.

Some of the recipes call for unassuming ingredients such as lentils, kohlrabi, and celery root. If you can cook cabbage, you can cook kohlrabi—so why not try it? The same holds for other foods. Take razor clams: The mollusk may be unfamiliar, but anyone who is comfortable with cherrystones or littlenecks can cook these.

Many of these recipes have evolved from very personal memories of my life, my travels, and other aspects of this great journey that defines my blessed career. Charred Lamb with Truffle Vinaigrette and Oven-Dried Tomatoes (page 144) transports me immediately to the south of France, where I first tasted its ingredients on one plate. I am fascinated by how cooking is a process of re-creating memories in the kitchen. Unlike the artist who has one shot at a particular painting or sculpture, the cook can conjure up a palette of tastes, colors, and textures many times over.

Some of these recipes require special equipment, but most ask only that you work with good, sharp knives and other basics, such as fine-mesh sieves, heavy saucepans, a heavy-duty blender, and a food processor. For the juices, you will need a juicer. This does not have to be a superexpensive model, but make sure it is a juice extractor—not a gizmo for squeezing citrus fruit. For the foams, you will need a foam canister, which can be found at fine kitchenware shops. And I highly recommend everyone invest in a mandolin, which will allow you to make exceptionally thin slices. No need to buy the most expensive—the plastic sort, called a Japanese mandolin, is perfect.

I find that half the fun of the *amuse-bouche* is in the presentation—good news for anyone who likes to poke around in antique stores, building-supply stores, garage sales, and Grandma's attic. It's gratifying and good fun to come up with oddball and unorthodox ways to serve these little jewels dramatically and playfully.

At Tru, I use pristine white plates, Asian-style bowls and spoons, sparkling shot glasses, sleek black trays, long-handled spoons and forks, mirrors, and granite and marble tiles. I sometimes serve small *amuse* in old-fashioned demitasse cups, finger bowls, heavy glass ashtrays, votive-candle holders, Depression juice glasses, and odd-sized cut-glass glasses, as well as on green-rimmed glass shelving, old-time wooden checkerboards, and small silver trays. I offer *soba* noodles, microgreens, and hamachi tartare on highly polished, mismatched flatware, and salads on diminutive colorful plates from Chinatown. As with the food, the sky is the limit here—get your party off to a charming start with quirky fun or old-school elegance.

amuse-bouche

soup*amuse*

spring

CHILLED ASPARAGUS SOUP
WITH CRÈME FRAÎCHE

----

serves 8

Ever since I tasted gazpacho, I have been a huge fan of all chilled soups, and none is better than one made with green or white asparagus. You can make this with the asparagus stems and save the tips for another use. Vegetable stock forms the base of the soup, which I garnish with pretty swirls of crème fraîche. The only other ingredients are orange juice and orange zest—tasty flavor accents with asparagus. I ladle the soup into demitasse or other small cups for a refreshing start to a meal.

1 pound green asparagus, trimmed and cut into 1½- to 2-inch pieces	Juice of 1 orange
2¼ cups Vegetable Stock (page 243) or water, plus more as needed	Salt
Grated zest of 1 orange	Crème fraîche, homemade (page 252) or store-bought, or sour cream, for garnishing

1. In a large pot of boiling water, blanch the asparagus for 5 to 10 minutes or until fork-tender. Drain and immediately submerge in cold water. Drain again.

2. Transfer about a quarter of the asparagus pieces to a blender and add about ½ cup of the stock. Puree until smooth. Pour into a larger bowl. Continue pureeing the remaining asparagus and stock in batches. Strain through a *chinois* or fine-mesh sieve into the bowl.

3. Stir the orange zest and juice into the soup. Gently stir in more stock until the soup is the consistency you prefer. Season to taste with salt. Cover and chill.

4. Serve the chilled soup in small bowls or demitasse cups, each garnished with a spoonful of crème fraîche.

CHILLED VELOUTÉ OF SUNCHOKES
WITH PICKLED SUNCHOKES
AND SEVRUGA CAVIAR

serves 10

Credit for this soup goes to Elliot Bowles, one of my former sous-chefs at Tru, who grew up in a military family and lived all over the world. He attributes his love for sunchokes to the years he spent in Hawaii. I had barely heard of them before I met Elliot and was bowled over when I tasted this soup. You will be, too. The sunchokes give it a mild nuttiness, somewhat like water chestnuts. I add the caviar for saltiness and elegance.

Sunchokes are also called Jerusalem artichokes and, despite this moniker, are tubers from a native American sunflower and are not related to artichokes. When you buy them, there is no hint of the glorious sunflower, but instead the chokes are beige-colored knobs that resemble fresh ginger. Like potatoes, they darken, or oxidize, when sliced, so keep them in acidulated water while you work. This recipe requires some preparation a day ahead.

1 tablespoon fresh lemon juice	Salt
7 sunchokes (Jerusalem artichokes)	²⁄₃ cup heavy cream
3 tablespoons Pickling Spice Blend (page 251)	¹⁄₃ cup Vegetable Stock (page 243), plus more as needed
1 cup Simple Syrup (page 251)	Freshly ground white pepper
¹⁄₂ cup white wine vinegar	1 tablespoon sevruga caviar

1. A day before you plan to serve this, fill a large nonreactive bowl with water and add 1 teaspoon of the lemon juice to make acidulated water.

2. Peel and cut the largest sunchoke into 10 thin slices, dropping the slices into the acidulated water as they are cut. This will prevent them from turning brown.

3. Cut an 8-inch square of cheesecloth and mound the pickling spices in the center of the square. Bring the corners of the cloth together and tie the sachet with kitchen string.

4. Combine the syrup and vinegar in a medium-sized glass or ceramic bowl. Drain the sunchoke slices and add to the bowl along with the spice sachet. Season to taste with salt. Cover and refrigerate for at least 24 hours.

5. Remove and discard the sachet and drain the sunchoke slices before serving.

6. Fill a large nonreactive bowl with water and add the remaining lemon juice to make acidulated water.

7. Peel and coarsely dice the remaining 6 sunchokes, dropping the dice into the acidulated water as they are cut.

8. Combine the cream and vegetable stock in a large saucepan. Drain and add the sunchoke dice. Bring to a boil over medium-high heat, reduce the heat, and simmer for 10 to 15 minutes or until the sunchokes are tender.

9. Transfer the soup to a blender and puree until smooth. You will have to do this in batches. Strain the batches through a *chinois* or fine-mesh sieve into a large bowl. Stir in more stock until the soup reaches the consistency you prefer. Season to taste with salt and white pepper. Cover and chill.

10. Serve the chilled soup in small bowls or demitasse cups with a slice of pickled sunchoke and a garnish of caviar.

CHILLED SWEET PEA SOUP

WITH LOBSTER

serves 6

Although I remember my grandmother's sweet pea soup with affection, she made it with bacon—lots of bacon—much like she made split pea soup. When I decided to make my own, I lightened it by eliminating the bacon, chilled it, and served it with mint. Delicious! But I couldn't leave well enough alone and so turned it into a seafood soup by adding lobster. More delicious! You could replace the lobster with crab or mussels, too.

Sweet peas are also called English or garden peas. Shell them right before making the soup to keep the peas from drying out. Remove any strings from the pods, slit the pods open, and then push out the little round peas with your thumb. If you must shell them ahead of time, wrap them in a damp towel and refrigerate for no more than a few hours.

One 2-pound lobster	1½ cups water, plus more as needed
4 cups shelled fresh sweet peas, 6 pea pods reserved	Salt and freshly ground white pepper

1. Plunge the lobster headfirst into a large pot of rapidly boiling salted water. Cover and boil for 8 to 12 minutes or until bright red and cooked through. Using a pair of long tongs, remove the lobster from the pot and immediately submerge in cold water. Drain the lobster and allow to cool.

2. When cool enough to handle, crack the lobster and remove the meat from the tail, claws, and knuckles. Put the meat into a bowl, cover, and refrigerate until thoroughly chilled. You should have about 6 ounces of lobster meat.

3. In a large pot of boiling water, blanch the peas for 2 to 5 minutes or until tender when bitten into. Drain and immediately submerge in cold water. Drain again.

4. Transfer half of the peas and ¾ cup of the water to a blender. Puree until smooth. Strain through a *chinois* or fine-mesh sieve into a large bowl. Puree the remaining peas and water and strain into the bowl. If needed, gently stir in more water until the soup reaches the consistency you prefer. Season to taste with salt and white pepper. Cover and chill.

5. Cut the lobster meat into 6 equal portions. Stuff each portion of meat into a reserved pea pod.

6. To serve, pour ¼ cup of the chilled soup into a small glass and straddle a filled pea pod on the rim of the glass. Repeat to make 5 more servings.

CHILLED FAVA BEAN SOUP
WITH SEARED SCALLOPS

serves 6

Fava beans are part of a springtime triumvirate, joining asparagus and peas as a cherished sign of the season. If you've never cooked them before, trying them in this amuse *is a good way to learn how and to involve your guests in the kitchen. You may find peeling the beans a pleasant, if fleeting, rite of spring, as I do. Searing brings out the scallops' sweetness, which complements the butteriness of the beans for a rich, intoxicating soup that can be served hot or cold. If you can find scallops in the shells, buy them, and then serve the soup directly in the delicate shells for a spectacular presentation.*

The first time I tasted fava beans and scallops together was at the legendary Swiss restaurant Fredy Giradet in the early 1990s. The restaurant was so remote, I had to take a plane, train, and automobile to get there, but the chef's cooking left me with the impression of a lifetime.

3 ounces shelled fresh sweet peas (see page 8)	1 tablespoon fresh orange juice
6 ounces shelled fresh fava beans, peeled (see Note)	Salt and freshly ground white pepper
¼ cup water, plus more as needed	6 sea scallops
2 tablespoons olive oil	Lobster roe, for garnishing
	Grated orange zest, for garnishing

1. In a large pot of boiling water, blanch the peas for 2 to 5 minutes or until done (to test for doneness, bite into a pea). Drain and immediately submerge in cold water. Drain again.

2. In a large pot of boiling water, blanch the peeled fava beans for 3 to 6 minutes or until done (to test for doneness, bite into a bean). Drain and immediately submerge in cold water. Drain again.

3. Transfer the peas and fava beans to a blender. Add the ¼ cup water and puree until smooth. Add 1 tablespoon of the oil and puree again until well combined. Strain through a *chinois* or fine-mesh sieve into a medium-sized bowl. If needed, gently stir in more water until the soup reaches the consistency you prefer. Stir in the orange juice and season to taste with salt and white pepper. Cover and chill.

4. Heat the remaining 1 tablespoon oil in a cast-iron skillet over high heat until almost smoking. Cook the scallops for about 2 minutes on each side or until well browned. Transfer to a plate.

5. To serve, pour about 2 tablespoons of the chilled soup into a small soup cup and top with a scallop half, seared side up. Garnish with lobster roe and orange zest. Repeat to make 5 more servings.

NOTE: To peel fava beans, remove the beans from the pods. Blanch them in boiling water for 1 minute. Drain and cool and when you are able to handle them comfortably, pinch the beans to remove the skins.

CARROT SOUP WITH
HAWAIIAN GINGER

serves 6

I traveled to Hawaii a few years ago to participate in the 2000 annual Cuisines of the Sun event held on the Big Island. While in the islands, I made sure to stop in Honolulu to eat at my friend's restaurant, Alan Wong's, where Alan is chef-owner. While there, I tasted an unbelievable carrot-and-ginger crème brûlée that Alan makes with pink ginger, which is young ginger with visible pink strands mingled with its cream-colored flesh. If you can find it, use it for this soup. It's sweeter and a little milder than the fresh ginger found in most supermarkets. If you can't get pink ginger, feel free to use the more common variety. I love how ginger offsets the natural sweetness of carrots.

1 tablespoon unsalted butter

½ cup chopped carrots

1 tablespoon fresh orange juice

2 teaspoons finely grated Hawaiian pink ginger or other fresh ginger

2 cups water

Salt and freshly ground black pepper

1. Melt the butter in a small saucepan over low heat. Add the carrots and cook, stirring occasionally, for about 8 minutes or until the carrots begin to soften without coloring.

2. Add the orange juice, ginger, and water. Increase the heat to medium and bring to a simmer. Reduce the heat to low and simmer gently for about 30 minutes or until the carrots are very soft. Remove the pan from the heat and set aside to cool slightly.

3. Transfer the soup to a blender and puree until smooth. Strain the soup through a *chinois* or fine-mesh sieve into a small bowl. Season to taste with salt and pepper. Reheat the soup in a small saucepan over medium heat if necessary.

4. Serve the warm soup in small bowls or demitasse cups.

ROASTED GARLIC SOUP
WITH LOVAGE

serves 8

Because it's so easy to roast garlic wrapped in foil, I do it often, squeezing the mild, sweet-tasting pulp onto toasted bread; I love to snack on it as I work. I thought the same flavor would work well in a creamy soup, particularly if garnished with lovage, an old-fashioned green not much used anymore. Lovage has a distinctly strong, celerylike flavor that melds nicely with the garlic. Never use too much or it will overpower a dish, but do try it in salads and stews and especially with game meat. You might have to search for lovage, although if you keep your eyes open, you can find it at farmers' markets and greengrocers. Lovage seeds are marketed as celery seed.

1 head garlic, unpeeled	1 cup water
2 tablespoons olive oil	Salt and freshly ground black
1 teaspoon chopped fresh thyme	pepper
1 tablespoon finely chopped onion	1/3 cup loosely packed fresh lovage
1 tablespoon finely chopped celery	leaves
1/2 cup heavy cream	

1. Preheat the oven to 325°F.

2. Slice the head of garlic in half horizontally, across the equator, and place the halves, cut side up, on a large square of aluminum foil. Drizzle the exposed garlic cloves with 1 tablespoon of the oil and sprinkle with the thyme. Wrap the halves securely in the foil and place on a small baking tray. Roast for about 30 minutes or until tender.

3. When cool enough to handle, extract the garlic cloves by gently squeezing the halves. Put the roasted garlic cloves in a small bowl and set aside.

4. Heat the remaining 1 tablespoon oil in a small saucepan over low heat. Add the onion and celery and cook, stirring occasionally, for about 5 minutes or until the vegetables have softened without coloring.

5. Add the extracted roasted garlic, the cream, and the water. Simmer for 30 minutes over low heat. Remove the pan from the heat and set aside to cool slightly.

6. Transfer the soup to a blender and puree until smooth. Strain through a *chinois* or fine-mesh sieve into a small bowl. Season to taste with salt and pepper. Reheat the soup in a small saucepan over medium heat if necessary.

7. Stack the lovage leaves on a work surface. Using a sharp knife, cut the stack lengthwise into very thin strips, discarding the central ribs.

8. Serve the warm soup in small bowls or demitasse cups and garnish each serving with lovage.

CHILLED CUCUMBER SOUP
WITH LEMON OIL

serves 6

This light, summery soup screams to me: "Let's start eating!" It does a great job of stimulat-ing the palate, priming it for the meal to come, as a successful amuse should. Everyone in the Tru kitchen knows how much I like cucumbers, so when they peel them for other dishes, they always save the green skins for me. I sprinkle them with a little lemon or lime juice and eat them right then and there. My appreciation for cucumbers comes from my mother, Glo-ria Tramonto, who grew them in her expansive vegetable garden every year. As any pickle lover knows, acid is great with cucumbers, and my acid of choice is citrus juice. Here, I call for English cucumbers, which, grown primarily in greenhouses, have few seeds and can be up to a foot long. Look for cukes with dark-green skin and as little yellowing as possible.

2 English cucumbers, peeled and cut into 1-inch pieces	Lemon Oil (recipe follows), for garnishing
¼ cup crème fraîche	Chopped chives, for garnishing
Salt	

1. Put the cucumber pieces in the bowl of a food processor and process until pureed. Add the crème fraîche and pulse. Season to taste with salt. Cover and refrigerate for 2 hours or until chilled.

2. To serve, divide the chilled soup among 6 small bowls or demitasse cups. Adjust the sea-soning. Garnish each serving with a few drops of lemon oil and a sprinkling of chives.

LEMON OIL

makes 1 cup

zest of 10 lemons, removed in strips	1 cup grapeseed oil

1. Put the zest and the oil in a small saucepan over low heat and bring to a simmer. As soon as the mixture comes to a simmer, remove from the heat and allow to steep for 2 hours.
2. Strain the lemon oil through a *chinois* or fine-mesh sieve into a small bowl or glass container. Cover and refrigerate for up to 2 weeks.

BLISTERED CORN SOUP
WITH WHITE CORN ICE

serves 6

I have always loved eating at New York restaurants, especially since Chef Bobby Flay opened his Mesa Grill. Bobby and I "grew up" together as line cooks in New York City in the early 1980s, and he remains a good friend. He does incredible things with blistered corn, including making a superb corn chowder. When I developed my own, I decided to add the corn ice to the soup. The hot and cold sensations are enticing, and if you aren't in the habit of experimenting with temperatures, this is a good place to start. This soup can be served chilled as well as hot.

1 tablespoon olive oil

1 cup fresh corn kernels (from 2 ears)

½ cup Vegetable Stock (page 243), plus more as needed

Salt and freshly ground black pepper

White Corn Ice (recipe follows), for garnishing

1. Heat the oil in a heavy-bottomed sauté pan or cast-iron skillet over high heat. When the oil is hot, sauté the corn kernels for 2 to 3 minutes or until charred and cooked through.

2. Combine the charred corn kernels with a small amount of the stock in a blender. With the motor running, add as much additional stock as necessary to obtain the consistency you prefer. Strain through a *chinois* or fine-mesh sieve into a small bowl. Season to taste with salt and pepper. Reheat the soup in a small saucepan over medium heat if necessary.

3. Serve the warm soup in small bowls or demitasse cups garnished with shavings of corn ice.

WHITE CORN ICE

6 cups fresh corn kernels	Salt
(from 12 ears)	Fresh lemon juice
2 ½ tablespoons sugar	

1. Juice the corn kernels in a juicer and pour the juice into a bowl. You should have about 4 cups of juice. Add the sugar and stir until dissolved. Season to taste with salt and lemon juice.

2. Put the juice into a small, shallow metal pan. Cover and freeze for about 45 minutes. Take the pan from the freezer and stir the ice with a fork to break it up. Return it to the freezer for about 3 hours longer or until frozen solid.

3. When ready to serve, scrape the frozen corn ice with a fork to garnish. Serve leftovers on their own as a palate refresher or even dessert.

serves 8

For most of the year, it's hard to imagine worrying about an overabundance of ripe, juicy, sun-kissed tomatoes, but happily this is the case in August and early September, particularly for denizens of the Midwest, where the tomatoes are superb. I eat them raw and cooked; I oven-dry and can them. Those that get a little overripe end up in this soup, which is as tempting hot as it is chilled—and which I have never thought should be relegated to quick lunches only. This is an easy recipe that can be multiplied three or four times over for larger servings. Alter the flavor a little by using cilantro or flat-leaf parsley instead of basil.

2 to 3 ripe tomatoes

1 tablespoon unsalted butter

1 tablespoon finely chopped onion

1 tablespoon finely chopped fresh
   basil, or 1½ teaspoons dried

Salt and freshly ground black pepper

Chopped fresh basil, for garnishing

1 tablespoon extra-virgin olive oil

1. Peel, core, and finely chop the tomatoes to measure 2 cups.

2. Melt the butter in a small saucepan over low heat. Add the onion and cook, stirring occasionally, for about 5 minutes or until the onion has softened but not colored.

3. Add the tomatoes and cook over low heat, partially covered, for 30 to 40 minutes or until the tomatoes are broken down and somewhat liquid. Stir occasionally while cooking. Stir in the 1 tablespoon of basil. Remove the pan from the heat and set aside to cool slightly.

4. Transfer the soup to a blender and puree until smooth. Strain through a *chinois* or fine-mesh sieve into a small bowl. Season to taste with salt and pepper. Reheat the soup gently if necessary.

5. Serve the warm tomato soup in small bowls or demitasse cups and garnish each serving with chopped fresh basil and a drizzle of olive oil.

FRENCH LENTIL SOUP
WITH BACON

serves 8

It's not surprising that I fell in love with French soups, such as onion and lentil, when I lived in England and was able to travel to France so often. My regular excursions gave credence to the old joke that the best thing about England is France! So many of those old-time, rustic soups are flavored with ham bones and other parts of the hog, pork cuts people shy away from nowadays. I understand why, but I also think it's a shame, since the pork provides such depth and pulls the flavors together. I use everyday bacon here, which admittedly is so tasty because it's about 50 percent fat! If you see a recipe calling for cured pork belly, you can use bacon—it's the same thing. For me, this soup is the ultimate comfort food. I like to serve it as an amuse, although it's wonderful in larger amounts. You can turn it into a meal by adding crabmeat, chicken, or rich Italian or Polish sausage. It's good eats!

1 ounce bacon, very finely diced	1/4 cup French green lentils, rinsed
1 tablespoon finely chopped onion	and drained
1 tablespoon finely chopped carrot	2 cups water
1 tablespoon finely chopped celery	Salt and freshly ground black pepper

1. Put the bacon in a small saucepan over low heat and cook until the fat is rendered and the bacon begins to cook. Increase the heat and continue to cook until the bacon is crisp and golden brown. Remove the bacon with a slotted spoon to a small plate and reserve. Leave the bacon fat in the pan.

2. Add the onion, carrot, and celery to the saucepan. Cook over low heat, stirring occasionally, for about 5 minutes or until the vegetables have softened but not colored.

3. Add the lentils and stir to coat with the fat. Cover with the water and bring to a boil. Reduce the heat and simmer, partially covered, for about 30 minutes or until the lentils are very tender. Remove the pan from the heat and set aside to cool slightly.

4. Transfer the soup to a blender and puree until smooth. Strain through a *chinois* or fine-mesh sieve into a small bowl. Season to taste with salt and pepper. Reheat the soup in a small saucepan over medium heat, if necessary.

5. Serve the warm soup in small bowls or demitasse cups and garnish each serving with some of the reserved bacon.

vegetable*amuse*

SALAD OF RADISH AND

FIDDLEHEAD FERNS

---

serves 6

I think of fiddleheads as the platypus of the vegetable kingdom: odd and wonderful. Regardless of where you live along the East Coast, fiddlehead ferns have a very short season. In northern regions, they are available for about two weeks in June, while in more southern reaches, their brief season falls in April. Fiddleheads are furled ferns, wound into bright green coils that resemble the spiraled end of a fiddle, with a fresh flavor that, like that of asparagus and peas, announces that spring has indeed arrived. Nearly all recipes call for cooking the fiddleheads, and while this one is no exception, I like to crunch on raw ones while I work in the kitchen.

Here, I pair paper-thin slices of peppery radish with the fiddleheads and serve the ferns as a small, tempting salad—nothing is prettier or fresher-looking after a long winter than these bright-green charmers. If home cooks try them at all, they usually blanch fiddleheads and serve them with butter. Were I to do this, I would also mince some shallot or scallion to toss with them.

½ pound fiddlehead ferns (about 16 fiddleheads)	Fresh lemon juice
2 tablespoons extra-virgin olive oil, plus more as needed	Fleur de Sel or other high-quality sea salt
15 red or black radishes	Bachelor's button flowers, for garnishing
Freshly ground black pepper	

1. Cut off the base from each fiddlehead if dry and brown. Rinse each fern well, rubbing off any brown chaff from the sides.

2. In a large pot of lightly salted boiling water, blanch the fiddleheads for 5 to 7 minutes or until just tender. Drain and immediately submerge in cold water. Drain again.

3. Remove the thick stem end of each fiddlehead and reserve. Put the coiled tops in a medium-sized bowl and set aside.

4. Puree the reserved fiddlehead stem ends in a food processor or blender. With the motor running, add as much water as needed for a saucelike consistency. Add the oil and process

until emulsified. For a thicker sauce, add another tablespoon or so of oil. Transfer to a small bowl.

5. Using a Japanese mandolin or a very sharp knife, cut the radishes into paper-thin slices and add to the bowl of fiddlehead tops. Add enough olive oil to lightly coat the salad. Season to taste with pepper, lemon juice, and Fleur de Sel.

6. To serve, place some of the salad on a small plate along with the sauce. Garnish with bachelor's buttons. Repeat to make 5 more servings.

TERRINE OF PENCIL GREEN ASPARAGUS
WITH GOAT CHEESE PUREE

serves 10 to 12

Making this terrine with thin, tender asparagus is almost like stacking Lincoln Logs—it's that easy. Yet when you cut into it, the symmetry and simplicity are dazzling. If you've never made a terrine before, this would be a good place to start. The trick is to get uniformly sized, pencil-thin stalks of spring's finest asparagus. I serve this with a goat cheese puree, but with a little extra effort, you could layer the asparagus with the goat cheese. The two flavors go hand in hand.

There are numerous kinds of goat cheeses available. American goat cheeses tend to be milder than the French varieties—I like Bûcheron, but you should choose your favorite. Check out local goat cheese producers. You'll find some good cheeses and support local farmers at the same time.

3 pounds very thin green asparagus, trimmed	½ cup water
2 cups Vegetable Aspic (page 250)	Salt and freshly ground black pepper
Nonstick cooking spray	Purple kohlrabi microgreens, chervil,
6 ounces Bûcheron or other high-quality goat cheese	or other pretty, small-leafed greens, for garnishing

1. Cut off the tender tips from the asparagus and reserve for another use. If the asparagus stalks are very slender, the ends won't need to be removed, but if a few appear tough or thick, break them where they naturally snap. Trim the stalks to the same length so they are easy to stack. Line them up at the tip ends to do so.
2. In a large pot of boiling water, blanch the asparagus stalks for 1 to 3 minutes or until fork-tender. Drain and immediately submerge in cold water. Drain again.
3. Put the vegetable aspic in a small saucepan and cook over low heat until just melted.
4. Lightly coat a long, shallow, 1-cup terrine mold, approximately 3 inches long and 2 inches wide, with nonstick cooking spray and line with plastic wrap, leaving 3-inch overhangs on the long sides of the terrine.
5. Make the first layer by laying the asparagus side by side in the terrine. Cut the stalks to fill

in a single layer so there are no gaps. Spoon just enough aspic over the asparagus to coat the stalks. Continue layering the asparagus and aspic until the terrine is filled. The final layer should be aspic. Place the mold on a rimmed tray to catch any overflow of juices. Fold the overhanging ends of the plastic wrap over the top of the terrine and set a piece of foil-lined lightweight cardboard, cut to fit inside the mold, on top of the plastic wrap. Place a weight, such as a soup can laid on its side, on top of the cardboard and refrigerate for at least 24 hours.

6.   Put the goat cheese and about 2 tablespoons of the water in a small saucepan. Cook over low heat, whisking constantly, until the mixture is smooth and just warm. Add as much of the remaining water as needed for a saucelike consistency. Season to taste with salt and pepper. Set aside, covered, to keep warm.

7.   To serve, use the plastic wrap to lift the terrine from the mold. Unwrap and cut the terrine into ½-inch slices. Spoon a pool of goat cheese puree in the middle of a small plate. Lay 1 slice of terrine on top. Garnish with greens and season to taste with salt and pepper. Repeat to make 9 to 11 more servings.

serves 6

If for no other reason, please make this amuse to discover the joy of shallots. The small onion has a subtler flavor than its more robust cousins, but one that shines through in sauces, salads, and this velvety bite of egg custard. The flavor only intensifies when the shallots are roasted. I also like this custard because it reminds me of quiche, the egg-custard pie that is considered old-fashioned nowadays. I credit my longtime friend Julia Child with raising my consciousness about quiche and, like her, I think it is superb. Nothing tastes better than a properly made quiche, and I would like nothing better than to see it regain popularity.

3 shallots	1 sprig fresh thyme
2 tablespoons olive oil	1½ large egg yolks (see Note)
Salt and freshly ground black pepper	1 tablespoon snipped fresh chives
½ cup heavy cream	

1. Preheat the oven to 350°F.

2. Peel and trim the shallots and put them in a baking dish small enough to hold them snugly in one layer. Coat them with the olive oil and season to taste with salt and pepper. Roast for 45 minutes to 1 hour or until deep golden brown and tender. Remove from the oven and allow the shallots to cool.

3. Reduce the oven temperature to 325°F.

4. Finely chop the shallots and set aside.

5. Combine the cream and thyme in a small saucepan and bring to a simmer over medium heat. Simmer gently for 5 minutes.

6. Strain the cream through a *chinois* or fine-mesh sieve into a small bowl. Discard the thyme. Season to taste with salt and pepper.

7. In another small bowl, whisk the egg yolks until blended. Gradually whisk in the hot cream.

8. Ladle the custard into six 1-ounce ovenproof ramekins. Distribute the roasted shallots evenly among the ramekins and top with a sprinkling of chives.

9. Put the filled ramekins in a small baking dish and place it in the oven. Pour enough hot

water into the baking dish to come halfway up the sides of the ramekins. Bake for 5 to 10 minutes or until the custards are set.

10. Allow the custards to cool in the water until the water turns tepid. Serve the custards at room temperature in the ramekins.

NOTE: To determine half an egg yolk, whisk a yolk in a small cup. Measure it and then remove half of that amount.

HEIRLOOM TOMATOES,
"PANZANELLA STYLE"

serves 6

Good memories are often the best teachers, and I have a mouthwatering remembrance of a classic Italian panzanella salad Chef Joe Decker served at Lettuce Entertain You's Chicago restaurant Avanzare, which means "to advance or go forward." I worked with Joe as a sous-chef when I first moved to Chicago and began working for Lettuce Entertain You. This pre-dated my four-year odyssey in Europe, and when I returned, Joe had moved on to other Lettuce restaurants and I became the chef of Avanzare. Much later, I opened Tru in the same space Avanzare had occupied—but now I was the chef-owner. I immediately remembered the salad but made the medley of tomatoes, bread, basil, and olive oil more upscale for Tru's fine-dining menu. When I serve it as an amuse, I mix tiny dice of red and yellow tomatoes, always seeking out the best and ripest heirloom varieties, and serve it with buttermilk crackers instead of bread. As Albert Einstein once said: "Imagination is more important than knowledge."

1 cup diced red and yellow tomatoes

1 tablespoon olive oil

Salt and freshly ground black pepper

1 tablespoon balsamic vinegar

6 large shavings Parmigiano-
    Reggiano cheese

6 Buttermilk Crackers (page 247) or
    high-quality store-bought
    crackers

Currant tomatoes on the vine,
    for garnishing

1. In a small bowl, toss the tomatoes with the olive oil. Season to taste with salt and pepper.
2. To serve, divide the tomato salad among 6 small plates and drizzle with the vinegar. Top each serving with a shaving of cheese, a cracker, and a few currant tomatoes.

WATERMELON CUBE
WITH AGED BALSAMIC VINEGAR

serves 6

This charming little amuse *is comprised of two ingredients, and when there are only two, they had better be the best there are! My good friend Jose Andres inspired me to make this* amuse *one summer when he visited from his Washington, D.C., restaurant, Jaleo, where he is the chef-partner. Look for ripe, seedless watermelons in the height of summer, when they are bursting with luscious sweetness. Tap their shells; they should sound hollow and feel firm, never soft or mushy. Next, buy the oldest balsamic vinegar that you can afford. You may have to purchase it at a gourmet shop, but once you discover the glories of 25-, 50-, or even 100-year-old balsamic vinegar, you will be hooked. This is not vinegar to sprinkle with abandon over lettuce or tomatoes, but instead a syrupy elixir to use sparingly. Just a drop or two provides flavor that is rich, mellow, sweet, and full—unlike any vinegar you have tasted before. When paired with watermelon, as I have here, it's heavenly.*

½ cup watermelon juice (see page 184)	About ½ pound seedless red or yellow watermelon flesh
Salt	Aged balsamic vinegar, for garnishing

1. Strain the watermelon juice through a *chinois* or fine-mesh sieve into a small measuring cup with a spout. Season to taste with salt.
2. Cut the watermelon flesh into six 1½-inch cubes.
3. Use the small end of a melon baller to remove a scoop of flesh from one side of each of the watermelon cubes, creating a small cavity for the juice.
4. To serve, place a watermelon cube, cavity side up, on each of 6 small plates and pour watermelon juice into the cavity. Garnish each serving with a drizzle of balsamic vinegar.

RED, GOLD, WHITE,

AND CANDY-STRIPED BEETS

WITH BEET JUICE REDUCTION

serves 6

If you don't have fun with this dish, you're not doing it right! Go wild with the many differ-ent beets out there. I took all I could find at a local farmers' market and made an extraor-dinary and colorful salad, which I later pared down for an amuse, *using colorful beets supplied by Tom Cornille and Sons, my produce vendor, with whom I have worked for more than a dozen years. I serve this in a small paper cup, like the ones you might find at a fast-food restaurant for ketchup or relish, and arrange the beets according to color and shape. This* amuse *is very much about visual appeal. The beet juice reduction provides a little extra kick. Because this holds well, you can make it ahead of time, or you can increase the amounts and take it along on your next picnic.*

2 cups red beet juice (see page 184)	3 baby candy-striped beets
3 baby red beets	½ cup olive oil
3 baby gold beets	Salt and freshly ground black pepper
3 baby white beets	Fresh thyme leaves, for garnishing

1. Put the beet juice in a small, heavy-bottomed saucepan and bring to a boil over medium-high heat. Reduce the heat to maintain a simmer and simmer for about 25 minutes or until the juice is reduced to ¾ cup. Remove from the heat.

2. Strain the reduction through a *chinois* or fine-mesh sieve into a small bowl. Cover and re-frigerate until needed.

3. Preheat the oven to 375°F. Line a jelly-roll pan with aluminum foil.

4. Rinse and dry the beets. Remove all but 1 inch of the stems (leaving on the roots and part of the stems prevents the beets from bleeding). Coat the beets with 1 tablespoon of the olive oil and place them on the jelly-roll pan.

5. Roast the beets for 30 to 40 minutes or until tender. To test for tenderness, insert a skewer or paring knife into one of the beets. If the skewer meets with no resistance, the beets are done.

6.   When the beets are cool enough to handle, cut off the roots and stems. If you wish, keep the stems on a few beets for presentation. Slip the skins off the beets with your fingers.

7.   Cut the beets into quarters and put them into a medium-sized bowl. Toss with the remaining olive oil and season to taste with salt and pepper.

8.   To serve, place a few assorted beet quarters inside a small cup, positioning the ones with stems near the top. Drizzle with the red beet juice reduction and garnish with thyme leaves. Repeat to make 5 more servings.

serves 6

Like most Americans, I grew up eating three-bean salad at picnics and other summertime get-togethers. This was in upstate New York, where we were spoiled by the amazing produce stocked by Wegman's, the incredible supermarket owned by my friend Danny Wegman. I updated the concept by using three types of fresh beans rather than the expected canned kidney, garbanzo, and green beans. Haricots verts, also called French beans, are slender dark-green beans; wax beans share all the characteristics of green beans but are yellow or purple, the yellow being commonplace and the purple more difficult to find. If need be, you can substitute the latter with fresh cranberry beans, which are cream-colored speckled with red, or pole beans. The beans taste great dressed with curry, which is a change from the expected sweet, vinegary dressing found on most three-bean salads.

5 ounces haricots verts

5 ounces yellow wax beans

5 ounces purple wax beans,
cranberry beans, or pole beans

6 tablespoons Curry Oil (recipe
follows), plus more for garnishing

Salt and freshly ground black pepper

1. In a large pot of boiling salted water, blanch the haricots verts for 4 to 8 minutes or until just tender. Drain and immediately submerge in cold water. Drain again.

2. In another large pot of boiling salted water, blanch the yellow wax beans for 4 to 8 minutes or until just tender. Drain and immediately submerge in cold water. Drain again.

3. Cut the tops off both the haricots verts and the yellow wax beans and cut the beans on an extreme bias into 1-inch pieces, discarding the tails.

4. Cut the tops off the purple wax beans and cut the beans on an extreme bias into paper-thin slices, discarding the tails.

5. Put all the beans into a medium-sized bowl and toss with the curry oil until coated. Season to taste with salt and pepper.

6. To serve, divide the salad among 6 small plates and arrange in a pyramid fashion. Garnish with a drizzle of curry oil.

CURRY OIL

2 tablespoons curry powder	½ cup olive oil
½ cup grapeseed oil	

1. Spread the curry powder in a dry skillet and toast over low heat, shaking the pan gently, for 40 to 50 seconds or until the curry powder begins to change color.
2. Add the oils to the skillet, raise the heat, and bring to a simmer. Immediately reduce the heat to very low and steep gently for 1 hour.
3. Remove the skillet from the heat and let the oil cool to room temperature. Transfer the oil to a lidded glass container and refrigerate for 2 to 3 days to give the flavors time to blend.
4. Strain the oil through a coffee filter into a clean glass container. Use immediately or cover and refrigerate for up to 2 months.

CARAMELIZED FENNEL
WITH CELERY ROOT

serves 6

Fennel is a wonderful vegetable, available from late fall through the winter, but it's not always used to its best advantage. My friend Chef Mario Batali, chef-owner of Babbo Ristorante e Enoteca, in New York City, cooked for me one night and served a delicious caramelized fennel salad, which, as soon as I tasted it, sent me hurrying back to the Tru kitchen to create my own version. Fennel's intrinsic nuttiness is highlighted when it's caramelized. I serve it with a little celery-root puree, which heightens the earthiness of the dish while giving it great depth of flavor. Celery root, which is common in Europe, is becoming increasingly popular here.

1 celery root	1 fennel bulb
½ cup water	¾ cup olive oil
¼ cup heavy cream	¼ cup chopped flat-leaf parsley
Salt and freshly ground black pepper	

1. Remove the stems and leaves from the celery root. Peel and coarsely dice the flesh.

2. Combine the water, cream, and celery root in a small saucepan. Bring to a simmer over medium-high heat. Reduce the heat and simmer gently for 15 to 25 minutes or until the celery root is tender. Remove from the heat and allow to cool slightly.

3. Transfer the mixture to a blender and puree until smooth. Strain through a *chinois* or fine-mesh sieve into a small bowl. Season to taste with salt and pepper. Set aside to cool.

4. Cut the stems and fronds off the fennel and discard the fronds. Cut the bulb in half lengthwise. Remove and discard the core at the base of each half and very thinly slice the halves.

5. Heat 1 tablespoon of the oil in a small sauté pan over medium heat. Add a small amount of the fennel and cook, stirring occasionally, for 10 to 15 minutes or until it is a deep golden brown and softened. Season to taste with salt and pepper. Remove the fennel from the pan and let cool. Cook the remaining fennel in small batches, adding more oil each time.

6. Put the fennel in a medium-sized bowl and toss with the parsley and enough of the remaining olive oil to coat.

7. To serve, spread a spoonful of the celery-root puree on a small plate. Top with some of the fennel salad. Repeat to make 5 more servings.

FOREST MUSHROOM TERRINE

serves 8 to 12

This dish looks complicated but is a breeze to make. I developed it to take the best advantage of the ever-changing selection of mushrooms we get at Tru from our many resourceful mushroom suppliers, but I also wanted to make a terrine easy enough to serve to 130 people as an amuse—*a concern not shared by most home cooks!*

This is not a layered terrine but rather a mosaic-style terrine, a technique that I think everyone can do. You pour the mixture into the terrine mold and you're done. If for some reason the terrine doesn't set up, scrape it into a bowl, add a few more softened sheets of gelatin, and start again. This is one of the beauties of mosaic terrines—it takes a lot to ruin them!

I use yellow chanterelles, white oyster mushrooms, orange lobster mushrooms, earthy brown morels and shiitakes. All are gorgeous, and when the terrine is sliced, the multitude forms a mosaic, almost like an Impressionist painting. The tiny drizzle of truffle vinaigrette kicks up the flavor. Supermarkets and greengrocers all over the country sell wonderful fresh mushrooms in all shapes and sizes. This is a great opportunity to try the unfamiliar or a sampling of your favorites.

½ pound shiitake mushrooms	2 tablespoons chopped flat-leaf
½ pound portabello mushrooms	parsley
½ pound oyster mushrooms	Nonstick cooking spray
½ pound morel mushrooms	Truffle Vinaigrette (page 244)
20 sheets gelatin	Minced fresh chives, for garnishing
4 cups Vegetable Stock (page 243)	Fleur de Sel or other high-quality
2 cloves garlic, minced	sea salt, for garnishing
2 shallots, minced	

1. Wipe the mushrooms clean, using a small brush to rid them of dirt if necessary. Remove the stems from the shiitake and portabello mushrooms. Remove the gills from the portabellos. Julienne the mushrooms.

2. Fill a large bowl with cold water. Gently drop the gelatin sheets into the water, several at a time, until all are submerged. Let soften and bloom for about 5 minutes.

3.   In a large saucepan, bring the stock to a simmer over medium-high heat. Using your hands, lift the gelatin sheets from the water and squeeze them gently between your fingers. Transfer the sheets to the hot stock. Stir gently until dissolved.

4.   Meanwhile, combine the minced garlic and shallots with the parsley.

5.   Put the mushrooms in a large bowl and scatter the garlic, shallots, and parsley over them. Pour the stock over the vegetables. Set aside for about 20 minutes to allow to cool to room temperature.

6.   Lightly coat a long, shallow, 3-cup terrine mold (I use a collapsible mold that is 20 inches long and 2 inches wide) with nonstick cooking spray and line with plastic wrap, leaving 3-inch overhangs on the long sides of the terrine.

7.   Lift the mushrooms from the gelled aspic with your hands or a large spoon. Spread in the terrine. Use your fingertips to push them into the bottom of the terrine in an even, tight layer. Spoon enough aspic over the mushrooms to reach the top of the terrine. Place the mold on a rimmed tray to catch any overflow of juices. Fold the overhanging ends of the plastic wrap over the top of the terrine and set a piece of foil-lined lightweight cardboard to fit inside the mold, on top of the plastic wrap. Place 2 or 3 weights, such as soup cans laid end to end, on top of the cardboard and refrigerate for at least 24 hours.

8.   To serve, use the plastic wrap to lift the terrine from the mold. Unwrap and cut the terrine into ¼-inch slices. Lay 1 slice on a small plate, drizzle with truffle vinaigrette, and garnish with minced chives and a sprinkling of sea salt. Repeat to make 7 to 11 more servings.

BRAISED KOHLRABI WITH BRUNOISE OF FALL VEGETABLES AND WHITE TRUFFLE EMULSION

serves 6

Most people don't know how to cook kohlrabi—and until I worked in London with renowned Swiss chef Anton Mosimann, I was unsure too. Kohlrabi is a root vegetable with edible leafy green tops. It's related to the turnip and, not surprisingly, tastes like one, only mellower. When I added the other root vegetables and the truffle emulsion to this dish, I realized it would make a superb fall amuse. This is a good way to try kohlrabi, although you can make it with small, tender turnips, too.

6 baby purple kohlrabi with their greens intact	Scant 2 tablespoons finely diced butternut squash
1 tablespoon unsalted butter	Scant 2 tablespoons finely diced parsnip
2 tablespoons olive oil	
Milk	1 teaspoon finely chopped flat-leaf parsley
Scant 2 tablespoons finely diced carrot	Salt and freshly ground black pepper
Scant 2 tablespoons finely diced potato	1 cup White Truffle Emulsion (recipe follows)
Scant 2 tablespoons finely diced rutabaga	

1. Cut the tops off the kohlrabi, keeping a little of the greens attached. Reserve both the tops and the bottoms.

2. In a large pot of boiling water, blanch the kohlrabi tops for 5 to 8 minutes or until the greens are barely wilted and the tops are fork-tender. Drain and immediately submerge in cold water. Drain again.

3. Put the butter and 1 tablespoon of the oil in a medium-sized saucepan over medium-high heat. When the oil is hot, add the kohlrabi bottoms and sauté for about 5 minutes or until nicely browned all over. Add enough milk and water, in equal parts, to cover the kohlrabi. Bring to a simmer over medium-low heat and cook for 10 to 15 minutes or until the bot-

toms are tender. Remove the pan from the heat. Drain and allow the kohlrabi to cool to room temperature.

4. Use the small end of a melon baller to remove a scoop of flesh from the cut side of each kohlrabi bottom to create a small cavity for stuffing. Set aside.

5. Heat the remaining 1 tablespoon oil in a small sauté pan over medium-high heat. Add the diced vegetables and sauté for about 5 minutes or until golden brown and tender.

6. Remove from the heat and toss with the parsley. Season to taste with salt and pepper.

7. To serve, spoon some of the truffle emulsion on a small plate. Lay a kohlrabi bottom over part of the emulsion and heap some of the diced fall vegetables into the hollowed-out cavity. Garnish with a kohlrabi top. Repeat to make 5 more servings.

WHITE TRUFFLE EMULSION

makes about 1¹/₂ cups

3 cups dry white wine	1¹/₂ cups heavy cream
2 small shallots, finely chopped	6 tablespoons unsalted butter
1 small sprig fresh thyme	1¹/₂ tablespoons white truffle oil
1 bay leaf	Salt and freshly ground white pepper

1. In a medium-sized, nonreactive saucepan, combine the wine, shallots, thyme, and bay leaf. Bring to a boil over medium-high heat. Reduce the heat and simmer for 30 to 35 minutes or until most of the wine has evaporated and the bottom of the pan is almost dry.

2. Add the heavy cream and bring to a boil. Remove from the heat and allow to steep at room temperature for 30 minutes.

3. Strain through a *chinois* or fine-mesh sieve into a bowl. Set the bowl in a larger bowl containing ice and ice water. Stir the *vin blanc* for about 10 minutes or until completely cool.

4. When cool, proceed immediately or cover the bowl with plastic wrap and refrigerate the *vin blanc* until needed. You will have about 2 cups of *vin blanc*.

5. Combine the *vin blanc*, butter, and truffle oil in a medium-sized saucepan. Bring to a simmer over medium-high heat, immediately remove the pan from the heat, and season to taste with salt and white pepper.

6. Using a handheld immersion blender, whip the mixture until foamy. Use the foamy top truffle emulsion immediately as desired.

NOTE: You use only the foamy bubbles for the emulsion. Because you need a volume of liquid to aerate this into foam, there will be extra liquid at the bottom of the saucepan. Discard it or use it as you wish.

RAPINI SALAD SCENTED
WITH NUTMEG

---

serves 6

I love rapini, and happily it's becoming more accepted here. Coming from a traditional Italian family, I grew up eating it with pleasure. My aunt, Dorothy Tramonto, is the queen of "rapi," as we called it at home. She prepares it with garlic, olive oil, chicken stock, and a little chili pepper and then finishes this much-praised family-style dish with a grating of Parmigiano-Reggiano cheese. I took my cue from her when I developed this contemporary warm winter salad as an amuse, *but added the nutmeg to update it. Rapini also answers to the name broccoli rabe.*

16 to 18 ounces rapini, trimmed	1 clove garlic, minced
2 tablespoons olive oil, plus more as needed	Salt and freshly ground black pepper
¼ cup thinly sliced shallots	Freshly grated nutmeg, for garnishing

1. Wash the rapini well in cold water and dry thoroughly. Cut the florets off the rapini and coarsely chop the stems and leaves. You should have enough to measure 2 cups.

2. Heat the oil in a medium-sized sauté pan over medium-high heat. Add the shallots and sauté for about 5 minutes or until softened and browned. Add the garlic and cook for an additional 1 to 2 minutes or until the garlic is fragrant. Add the rapini and additional olive oil as needed and sauté for about 5 minutes or until just wilted. Season to taste with salt and pepper.

3. Remove from the heat and divide the rapini among 6 small plates. Drizzle each salad with additional olive oil and garnish with freshly grated nutmeg. Serve warm.

CARROT CRÈME BRÛLÉE

WITH BLOOD ORANGE REDUCTION

AND CARROT SPROUTS

serves 10

Not many people would think of pairing carrots with cream, but when I was traveling in the south of France, I ate in Nice with Chef Jacques Maximim, who, with a dish he made, inspired me even further—to flavor creamed carrots with orange juice. At first, I wanted to make creamed carrot parfaits as an amuse, but when I tried this carrot flan, I abandoned the parfait idea. The flan, which can be made a few days ahead and cut into any shapes you like, explodes in the mouth with rich carrot flavor and a soft, silken texture—the perfect vehicle for a super little amuse.

Because I particularly like carrot and orange together, I use a blood orange reduction to garnish these amuse, but you can use any reduction you like. You can even make the flan with asparagus or broccoli instead of carrots. If you have a blowtorch, sprinkle sugar on top of the cutout shapes and caramelize them for the crème brûlée effect. Doing so adds another dimension that will surely impress your guests.

3 ¾ cups blood orange juice (see page 184)	2 tablespoons granulated sugar
1 ¼ cups carrot juice (see page 184)	7 sheets gelatin
1 ¾ cups plus 2 tablespoons chilled heavy cream	Nonstick cooking spray
1 pound carrots, peeled, trimmed, and coarsely grated	Coarse or granulated sugar (optional)
	Carrot sprouts, for garnishing

1. Put 2¼ cups of the blood orange juice in a small, heavy-bottomed saucepan and bring to a boil over medium-high heat. Reduce the heat and simmer for about 25 minutes or until the juice is reduced to ¾ cup.

2. Strain the reduction through a *chinois* or fine-mesh sieve into a small bowl. Cover and refrigerate until needed.

3. Put the carrot juice in a small, heavy-bottomed saucepan and bring to a boil over medium-

high heat. Reduce the heat and simmer for about 15 minutes or until the juice is reduced by half. Remove from the heat.

4. Put all but 3 tablespoons of the heavy cream in a large saucepan with the grated carrots, the 2 tablespoons granulated sugar, the carrot reduction, and the blood orange reduction and bring to a boil. As soon as the mixture comes to a boil, remove from the heat.

5. Meanwhile, fill a large bowl with cold water. Gently drop the gelatin sheets into the water, several at a time, until all are submerged. Let soften and bloom for about 5 minutes.

6. Transfer the carrot mixture to a blender and puree. You will have to do this in batches. Strain each batch through a *chinois* or fine-mesh sieve into a large bowl.

7. Using your hands, lift the gelatin sheets from the water and squeeze them gently between your fingers. Transfer the sheets to the still-warm carrot mixture and stir gently until dissolved. Allow to cool to room temperature.

8. In a chilled bowl with a chilled whisk, whip the remaining 3 tablespoons cream until firm peaks form. Fold the whipped cream into the carrot mixture.

9. Lightly coat a small jelly-roll pan, or other rimmed metal pan measuring about 9 by 12 inches, with nonstick cooking spray. Spoon in the carrot mixture. Smooth the surface and refrigerate, uncovered, for about 4 hours or until set. When the flan has set, cover with plastic wrap and keep refrigerated until ready to use.

10. Strain the remaining 1½ cups blood orange juice through a *chinois* or fine-mesh sieve into a small, heavy-bottomed saucepan and bring to a boil over medium-high heat. Reduce the heat and simmer for about 45 minutes or until reduced to ¼ cup. Remove from the heat and allow to cool. Cover and refrigerate until needed.

11. Using a small cookie cutter, cut the carrot flan into shapes. Gently lift the shapes from the flan with a small offset spatula and dip in the coarse sugar. Move a blowtorch over the cutout shapes for a few seconds or until the sugar caramelizes, if desired. Be careful not to hold the torch in one spot or too close, or you could melt the flan.

12. To serve, put 2 or 3 of the shapes on a small plate and drizzle with a little blood orange reduction. Garnish with carrot sprouts. Repeat to make 9 more servings.

WARM ONION TART
WITH THYME

serves 6

While this is a tasty little amuse, *another version I made at Brasserie T was also delicious. (A similar recipe for it is in my 1997 book,* American Brasserie.*) As much as I love the style of cooking we do at Tru, I am equally fond of a more informal style, such as that practiced at brasseries and trattorias. This makes sense, since I was trained in French country cooking and grew up in a family that was passionate about Italian country food. Someday I would love to open another casual-dining restaurant. When I worked in London, I was happily involved with the reopening of the Criterion Brasserie in Piccadilly Circus, which is housed in a landmark building and has existed on and off for generations. You may recall that it was at the very real Criterion that the fictional Sherlock Holmes met Watson to discuss his cases.*

These little warm onion tarts are lovely amuse *and get any winter meal off to a good start. Vary them with different kinds of onions. Julia Child has commented that cooking would be in a sorry state indeed if it weren't for onions. I agree!*

1 Spanish onion	Salt and freshly ground black pepper
1 tablespoon unsalted butter	1 sheet frozen puff pastry, thawed
1 tablespoon fresh thyme leaves	according to package directions

1. Peel and cut the onion in half through the root. Trim the ends and then julienne the onion lengthwise.
2. Melt the butter in a small sauté pan over medium heat. Add the onion and thyme and cook, stirring occasionally, for 10 to 15 minutes or until the onion is a deep golden brown. Season to taste with salt and pepper. Keep warm until ready to serve.
3. Meanwhile, preheat the oven to 400°F.
4. Unfold the puff pastry sheet on a lightly floured work surface and turn over to prevent the creases from splitting. Pat down gently to flatten the sheet.
5. Using a 1-inch round fluted cookie cutter, stamp out 6 rounds and transfer to an ungreased baking sheet. Bake for 8 to 10 minutes or until puffed and golden brown.

6.   Transfer the rounds to a wire rack to cool. When cool enough to handle, use a serrated knife to split each round in half horizontally.

7.   Assemble the tarts on small plates by spooning a generous amount of the warm onion mixture onto each of the bottom halves. Replace the tops and serve immediately on small plates.

AMARANTH WITH PICKLED RAMPS AND RAMP PUREE

serves 6

This amuse *evolved because I was looking for a way to use ramps, one of springtime's treats. Also called wild leeks, ramps resemble scallions and grow wild in the northern tier of the country. They taste at once like onions and garlic, and while their flavor is a little stronger than either, they can be served raw or cooked. I like them pickled, too. Ramps appear in farmers' and specialty markets in the early springtime and can be found as late as June. Use them soon after buying, but if you must, store them in the refrigerator wrapped in a cloth.*

I pair flavorful ramps with amaranth, an ancient grain used extensively by the Aztecs. The tiny golden grain has a crunchy texture and an unmistakably peppery flavor that begs for the company of oniony ramps. It's wonderful to cook with little-known grains such as amaranth, kamut, and spelt. They provide lovely flavor while delivering a good dose of protein and vitamins. Amaranth has been around for centuries, and while it may not be mass produced in the way wheat and corn are, it's not particularly hard to find in super-markets and natural food stores if you keep your eyes open. I really like the idea that it has been nurturing people for so long—and what better introduction than in a tasty amuse?

4 cups chopped ramp leaves	1 cup amaranth
2 tablespoons water	2 tablespoons olive oil
2 tablespoons grapeseed oil	1 cup Pickled Ramps (recipe follows)
Salt and freshly ground black pepper	

1. Put the ramp leaves and the water in a heavy-duty blender or food processor and puree. With the motor running, add the grapeseed oil and blend until emulsified. Season with salt and pepper as you work. Strain through a *chinois* or fine-mesh sieve into a small bowl. Taste and adjust seasoning. Cover with plastic wrap and chill.

2. Bring a medium-sized saucepan of water to a boil over high heat. Add the amaranth and cook for 8 to 10 minutes or until tender. Drain in a fine-mesh sieve and then carefully sub-merge the sieve in a bowl of cold water. Drain again and transfer to a bowl. Cover with plas-tic wrap and chill.

3. Toss the chilled amaranth with the olive oil and season to taste with salt and pepper.

4. To serve, spoon some of the chilled ramp puree onto a small plate. Place a portion of the amaranth on the plate along with a small amount of pickled ramps. Repeat to make 5 more servings.

PICKLED RAMPS

makes about 1 cup

1 bunch ramp leaves	½ cup Simple Syrup (page 251)
1 bunch fresh thyme, stemmed and leaves chopped	¼ cup white wine vinegar
1 tablespoon Pickling Spice Blend (page 251)	Salt

1. Cut enough of the ramp leaves into enough large squares to measure 1 cup and put them into a medium-sized glass or ceramic bowl.
2. Cut an 8-inch square of cheesecloth. Put the chopped thyme leaves and the pickling spices in the center of the cheesecloth and bring the corners together. Tie the sachet with kitchen string.
3. Put the simple syrup, vinegar, and spice sachet in a small, nonreactive saucepan. Season to taste with salt. Bring to a boil over medium-high heat. As soon as the mixture boils, reduce the heat and simmer for about 5 minutes. Remove and discard the sachet. Pour the hot liquid over the ramp leaves. Set aside to cool at room temperature for 1 hour. Cover and refrigerate until chilled.
4. Drain the ramps before serving.

serves 12 to 16

My first head-chef position was in 1987 at a Chicago restaurant called Bella Luna, where we served contemporary northern Italian food. I developed a four-inch frittata, served simply with a spicy tomato-basil sauce as an appetizer. I was eager to share it with customers, since I had only recently learned to love frittatas during a three-week driving trip from Paris to Rome; we ate them daily, at trattorias and small cafés, frittatas with cheeses, herbs, artichokes, olives, or tomatoes, served warm or at room temperature. I have transferred my appreciation for frittatas to this amuse *made with delicate angel hair pasta and artichoke hearts and then topped with small dollops of sumptuous crème fraîche.*

2 ounces angel hair pasta	Grated Parmigiano-Reggiano cheese,
3 large eggs	for garnishing
¼ cup milk	Chopped fresh herbs, such as
1 teaspoon baking powder	tarragon or basil with parsley and
2 tablespoons olive oil	chives, for garnishing
3 ounces artichoke hearts, quartered	6 tablespoons crème fraîche,
Salt and freshly ground black pepper	homemade (page 252) or store-
	bought

1. Preheat the oven to 450°F.

2. In a large pot of lightly salted boiling water, cook the pasta for 2 to 3 minutes or until al dente. Drain and immediately submerge in cold water. Drain again. Set aside.

3. In a small bowl, whisk the eggs until blended. Whisk in the milk and baking powder.

4. Heat the olive oil in an 8-inch ovenproof nonstick skillet over medium heat. Add the pasta and artichoke hearts and toss to mix. Using a spatula, spread the mixture evenly in the pan and then pour the eggs over it, making sure they completely cover the pasta. Cook for 2 to 3 minutes or until the eggs are set on the bottom. Season to taste with salt and pepper.

5. Transfer the skillet to the oven and bake for 2 to 4 minutes or until the eggs are completely cooked through. Remove from the oven and transfer the frittata to a flat plate.

6. Sprinkle with grated cheese and chopped fresh herbs and let the frittata stand for about 5 minutes before slicing into 12 to 16 wedges.

7. Serve immediately on small plates. Top each serving with crème fraîche.

RICOTTA-STUFFED RIGATONI

WITH SPRING VEGETABLES

AND PESTO OIL

serves 6 to 10

This simple idea came after a stage I did with my friend Chef Jean-Pierre Vigato, who is chef-owner of the critically acclaimed Paris restaurant Apicius. He made an amazing vegetable side dish by piping different mousses into rigatoni. At my restaurant, I stuff the rigatoni with herbed ricotta cheese and serve blanched vegetables on the side for a light, refreshing amuse. My customers love it. The trick is to cook the rigatoni only until al dente and then refrigerate it. This technique keeps it firm so it doesn't tear when it's stuffed, although you will note that I suggest cooking extra pasta because some inevitably split in the boiling water and others are lost to snacking!

1 cup rigatoni	1 yellow summer squash
Extra-virgin olive oil	1 cup green beans
1 cup whole-milk ricotta cheese	½ teaspoon fresh lemon juice
4 large fresh basil leaves, finely chopped	1 plum tomato, diced
Salt and freshly ground black pepper	Pesto Oil (page 246), for garnishing

1. In a large pot of lightly salted boiling water, cook the pasta for 11 to 14 minutes or until al dente. Drain and transfer to a medium-sized bowl, toss with a little olive oil to prevent sticking, and allow to cool slightly. Cover and refrigerate.

2. Stir the ricotta and basil together until well mixed. Season to taste with salt and pepper. Cover and refrigerate.

3. Slice the ends off the squash. Using a Japanese mandolin fitted with the fine-shredding blade, julienne lengthwise, avoiding the seedy center parts. If you don't have a mandolin, shred the vegetables as thinly as possible with a small, sharp knife.

4. In a saucepan of boiling salted water, cook the green beans for 3 to 4 minutes or until crisp and tender. Drain and immediately submerge in cold water. Drain again and set aside.

5. In another saucepan of boiling salted water, blanch the shredded squash for 1 minute.

Drain and immediately submerge in cold water. Drain again. Put the squash in a medium-sized bowl and set aside.

6. Toss the squash and green beans with 1 tablespoon oil, lemon juice, and salt and pepper to taste.

7. Fill a pastry bag fitted with a ⅓-inch plain tip with the ricotta filling. Pipe some of the filling into each rigatoni tube and arrange on a flat plate. (The cup of uncooked rigatoni will provide more than enough tubes of pasta. Use those that have not split during cooking.)

8. To serve, center a small mound of the squash and beans on a small plate. Top with a filled rigatoni tube, sprinkle with tomatoes, and drizzle with pesto oil. Repeat to make 5 to 9 more servings.

BULGUR SALAD WITH WATERCRESS
AND TOASTED WALNUT PUREE

serves 6

The more I use bulgur, the more I appreciate it. It's not actually a grain but instead wheat that has been steamed, dried, and cracked. For some recipes, like this one, it's cooked, but for others, it's soaked until tender. Once softened, it should be mixed with ingredients that emphasize its nuttiness, which is why I pair it here with walnut puree. It's one of the most forgiving grains to work with—you will find it much easier to cook than familiar rice.

½ cup chopped onions	Extra-virgin olive oil
¼ cup chopped carrot	Salt and freshly ground black pepper
¼ cup chopped celery	¼ cup toasted walnuts
½ cup bulgur	1 bunch watercress, for garnishing

1. Cut a 10-inch square of cheesecloth and place the onions, carrot, and celery in the center of the square. Bring the corners of the cloth together and tie the sachet with kitchen string.

2. Put the bulgur and vegetable sachet in a large pot of lightly salted boiling water. Reduce the heat and simmer for 10 to 12 minutes or until the bulgur is just tender. Drain in a colander and discard the sachet. Allow to cool, then transfer about 1 cup of the bulgur to a bowl.

3. Toss the cup of bulgur with as much olive oil as needed to coat the grains lightly. Season to taste with salt and pepper.

4. In a food processor, fitted with the metal chopping blade, or blender, puree the toasted walnuts with 3 to 4 tablespoons of olive oil until chunky-smooth.

5. Remove and discard the stems from the watercress. Reserve the leaves.

6. To serve, place about 2 tablespoons of the bulgur salad on each of 6 small plates along with some of the walnut puree. Garnish each serving with watercress leaves.

STRIPED FARFALLE
PASTA SALAD

serves 6

Salads are one of my all-time favorite ways to eat pasta. Pasta salads are simple but end-lessly versatile; you can dress them up with great olive or truffle oil, or leave them rustic. My culinary partner and pastry chef, Gale Gand, brought me several packages of tricolored, striped farfalle from Italy one year. Charmed by its appearance, I immediately went to work to develop a salad that could show it off. I generally serve a single-colored pasta for this amuse, but for the photograph opposite, I used tricolored farfalle. You can use any shade you like or stick with plain farfalle. For this salad, use fruity olive oil, voluptuous pancetta sliced paper thin, and the best aged Parmigiano-Reggiano cheese you can get. The cheese is shaved over the salad, so be sure to buy it in a hard chunk.

1 cup farfalle (bow-tie pasta)	2 cups mizuna leaves or other tender
5 tablespoons extra-virgin olive oil	greens
5 ounces pancetta, sliced paper thin	4 ounces Parmigiano-Reggiano
2 tablespoons fresh lemon juice	cheese, in one block
Salt and freshly ground black pepper	¼ cup grated lemon zest

1. In a large pot of boiling salted water, cook the pasta for 10 to 12 minutes or until al dente. Drain and immediately submerge in cold water. Drain again. Put into a large bowl and toss with 1 tablespoon of the olive oil. Set aside at room temperature to cool.

2. Meanwhile, preheat the oven to 300°F.

3. Arrange the pancetta slices in a single layer on a rimmed baking sheet. Bake for 10 to 15 minutes or until crisp. Cut the slices into large dice and transfer to a small bowl. Cover the bowl and refrigerate if you don't plan to use right away.

4. In a small bowl, whisk together the lemon juice and remaining 4 tablespoons of olive oil until blended. Season to taste with salt and pepper.

5. Add as much of the dressing as needed to coat the farfalle. Toss with the mizuna and pancetta.

6. To serve, center a small mound of the pasta salad on a small plate. Using a vegetable peeler, garnish the salad with shavings of the Parmigiano-Reggiano cheese. Garnish with lemon zest. Repeat to make 5 more servings.

serves 6

After becoming almost addicted to the duck wonton soup served at Lettuce Entertain You's Big Bowl restaurant and inspired by my friend chef-writer Bruce Cost, I decided to introduce something similar to Tru. We serve very little Asian food, although a number of our flavor combinations are inspired by the great cuisines of the East. Serving this as an amuse *seemed the perfect way to include it in Tru's repertoire. I present the little swallow of soup in an upside-down eggcup with a single wonton swimming in clarified duck broth. Wontons are lots of fun to work with—you can fill them with nearly anything—and make great hors d'oeuvres. Buy the wrappers in the produce section of the supermarket; freeze any extras.*

1 pound boned duck meat, trimmed of fat	4 large egg whites
2 onions, coarsely chopped	1 tablespoon white wine vinegar
2 carrots, coarsely chopped	4 cups Duck Stock (page 242)
2 ribs celery, coarsely chopped	6 Duck Wontons (recipe follows)
	Chopped fresh chives, for garnishing

1. Put the duck meat, onions, carrots, and celery in a meat grinder fitted with the coarse blade, or a food processor fitted with the metal chopping blade. Grind until coarse and then transfer to a stockpot.

2. Add the egg whites and mix until thoroughly incorporated. Stir in the vinegar. Whisking constantly, slowly pour in the duck stock.

3. Still whisking constantly, bring the liquid to a simmer over low heat. As soon as a coagulated froth (called a raft) forms on the surface of the liquid, stop whisking. Use the handle of a wooden spoon to poke a hole through the raft so that the stock can bubble through the hole without breaking the raft. Cook at a bare simmer, undisturbed, for 1 hour. At the end of the cooking time, the raft will be a solid crust and the consommé will be clear.

4. Line a *chinois* or fine-mesh sieve with several layers of moistened cheesecloth or a large coffee filter and set over a large pot. Ladle the consommé through the hole in the raft into the lined sieve, being careful not to break up the raft more than necessary so that very little of it mixes with the consommé, and strain. Allow the consommé to cool, then cover and refrigerate until needed. Discard the raft.

5.   To serve, gently heat about 2 cups of the consommé in a small saucepan. Do not let it boil. Place a duck wonton in each of 6 small heated bowls. Ladle a generous ⅓ cup of the consommé over each wonton and garnish with a sprinkling of chives.

DUCK WONTONS

makes 6 wontons

1 boned duck breast, skin on	2 tablespoons organic soy sauce
(8 to 10 ounces uncooked)	1 tablespoon sesame seeds
2 teaspoons vegetable oil	Salt and freshly ground black pepper
1 scallion, finely chopped	Six 3-inch round wonton wrappers
2 tablespoons sesame oil	

1.   Preheat the oven to 350°F.

2.   Put the duck breast in a baking pan and roast for 10 to 15 minutes or until medium-rare. Allow to cool at room temperature.

3.   Finely dice enough of the duck meat to measure ¾ cup. Save any remaining meat for another use; it freezes nicely if well wrapped and stored in a freezer-safe plastic bag.

4.   Heat the vegetable oil in a small sauté pan over medium heat. Add the scallion and cook, stirring, for about 3 minutes or until softened. Remove the pan from the heat and add the duck meat, sesame oil, soy sauce, and sesame seeds. Toss to combine and then transfer to a small bowl. Season to taste with salt and pepper. Set aside to cool.

5.   Lay the wonton wrappers on a work surface. Put 1 tablespoon of the filling in the center of each wrapper. With a small pastry brush or your index finger, moisten the edges of the wrapper with water. Fold the wrapper in half to form a semicircle and press the edges together to seal. (If you want, make extra wontons with the extra filling and freeze them. No need to defrost them before cooking.)

6.   Bring a large pot of water to a boil. Add the wontons and cook for 3 to 5 minutes or until cooked through and the wontons bob to the surface of the pot. Remove the wontons with a slotted spoon or spider and serve immediately.

SOFT POLENTA WITH FOREST MUSHROOMS

serves 6 to 10

Most people are potato crazed; I am polenta crazed! Soft polenta is as versatile as mashed potatoes—mix it with cheese, mushrooms, vegetables, even lobster. The key is to add enough butter so that it's irresistibly rich and yummy. I remember once eating soft polenta with roast pork at Chef Gualtiero Marchesi's three-star Michelin restaurant in Milan, Italy, in the early 1990s, and when we asked for seconds, they brought the pot from the kitchen and scooped the golden polenta straight onto our plates.

Polenta is cornmeal cooked with liquid—usually water or stock—until it thickens. A careful cook stirs it with a wooden spoon, never altering the direction of the stir. Soft polenta has the consistency of hot cereal, while firm polenta, which is cooked with less liquid, cools to form a firm, sliceable block. In Italy, firm polenta is traditionally sliced with a length of taut string. Both types of polenta can be sautéed, grilled, baked, or fried and served as a side dish or as part of a main course. I like to serve it as an amuse with a tumble of earthy mushrooms cooked with shallots until softened. When you select polenta meal for this recipe, try to buy a good imported brand. If you cannot find it, substitute stone-ground domestic cornmeal. Try not to buy instant polenta, which never achieves quite the desired consistency. Of course, if you put enough cheese and butter on anything, it tastes good!

½ cup polenta meal or cornmeal	2 shallots, finely chopped
2 ½ cups heavy cream	1 bay leaf
2 tablespoons grapeseed oil	3 tablespoons dry white wine
¼ cup chopped shiitake mushrooms	Salt and freshly ground black pepper
¼ cup chopped black trumpet or chanterelle mushrooms	3 tablespoons grated Parmigiano-Reggiano cheese, or more
¼ cup chopped oyster mushrooms	2 tablespoons unsalted butter
2 cloves garlic, finely chopped	

1. Put the polenta meal and cream in a large saucepan and bring to a boil over medium-high heat. Reduce the heat to low and simmer for 45 minutes, stirring occasionally to prevent the bottom from burning.

2. Heat the oil in a large sauté pan over medium-high heat. When the oil is hot, add the mushrooms and sauté for 10 to 15 minutes or until the mushrooms are browned and softened. Add the garlic, shallots, and bay leaf and cook for an additional 3 minutes or until the garlic and shallots are softened. Add the white wine while stirring the bottom of the pan with a wooden spoon to dissolve any browned solids into the liquid.

3. Remove from the heat, remove and discard the bay leaf, and season to taste with salt and pepper. Cover to keep warm.

4. Add the cheese and butter to the warm polenta. Stir until the butter melts and the cheese is incorporated. Taste and add more cheese, if desired.

5. To serve, arrange a mound of polenta on a small plate. Top with some of the mixed mushroom sauté. Repeat to make 5 to 9 more servings.

CREAMY CORN GRITS WITH BUTTERNUT SQUASH AND SWEET CORN

serves 6

When I was a kid, my maternal grandmother, who was from Abruzzi, Italy, lived with us and regularly cooked polenta. When I got older and began taking cooking seriously, I discovered that southern grits were similar to polenta, both being "poor man's foods." As I started to eat my way around the world, one of the best grits dishes I had was with my friend Chef Dean Fearing at the Mansion on Turtle Creek restaurant in Dallas, Texas. Both grits and polenta are forgiving: It's hard to overcook them and they carry a variety of flavors brilliantly. Here, I add Cheddar cheese to grits, as a play on the Parmigiano-Reggiano my grandmother might have used when cooking polenta. I tweak the flavor a bit by calling for fresh corn kernels to complement the corn grits. Because it is in season, I use butternut squash; this dish seems to belong in the winter. You could also add mushrooms, turnips, chicken or shrimp to make this a more substantial dish, or leave it as is: a small, hot amuse that will surprise and please your guests with its simplicity and humble origins.

1 butternut squash, peeled and diced (about 1 cup)	2 tablespoons grated Parmigiano-Reggiano cheese, plus more for garnishing
1 cup fresh corn kernels (from 2 ears)	2 tablespoons snipped fresh chives
2½ cups milk	Salt and freshly ground black pepper
2 tablespoons minced onion	Pinch of cayenne pepper
1 teaspoon minced garlic	Cracked black pepper, for garnishing
½ cup yellow corn grits	
½ cup shredded white Cheddar cheese	

1. | In a large saucepan of boiling water, blanch the squash for about 5 minutes or until just tender. Remove with a slotted spoon and set aside to cool.

2. | Let the water return to a boil and add the corn kernels. Blanch for 50 to 60 seconds, drain, and set aside to cool.

3. In a medium-sized saucepan, heat the milk, onion, and garlic over medium-high heat until scalding. Adjust the heat so that the milk simmers. Slowly add the grits, stirring with a wooden spoon until well mixed.

4. Cook over low heat, stirring constantly, for 12 to 15 minutes or until the grits reach the mush stage.

5. Remove the pan from the heat and stir in the cheeses and the chives. Season with salt and pepper.

6. To serve, arrange a mound of grits in a small bowl. Garnish with butternut squash and corn. Sprinkle Parmigiano-Reggiano cheese and cracked black pepper over the grits. Repeat to make 5 more servings.

CINNAMON FRENCH TOAST WITH
TURNIPS AND PRUNES

serves 6

There's a pancake house in Chicago called Walker Brothers—one of those places with lines out the door on weekend mornings—where I take my son, Gio, for breakfast. It's well known for its apple pancakes and cinnamon French toast, which father and son both love. Once, when I was preparing a special Mother's Day brunch at Brasserie T, the restaurant I owned several years before I opened Tru, I decided to offer cinnamon French toast on the menu. To make it more lunch-y than breakfast-y, I piled roasted turnips and prunes on top. Everyone in the kitchen thought I was out of my mind, but the customers loved it.

I tried this combination in the first place because of an incredible duck dish with turnips and prunes that Alfred Portale, one of my culinary mentors, made at Gotham Bar and Grill in New York City when I worked there in the late 1980s. At Tru, I serve this with orange brandy syrup as a beautiful amuse. It's magic.

½ cup pitted prunes	1 tablespoon unsalted butter
1 tablespoon grated orange zest	1 cup milk
½ cup brandy	1 large egg
¼ cup Simple Syrup (page 251)	Pinch of ground cinnamon
Salt	Six ¼-inch-thick slices Brioche
4 ounces baby turnips with their	(page 248)
greens intact	

1. Combine the prunes, orange zest, brandy, and simple syrup in a small saucepan. Season to taste with salt. Bring to a gentle boil over medium-high heat. Reduce the heat and simmer gently, partly covered, for about 20 minutes or until the prunes are plump and tender but not mushy.

2. Using a slotted spoon, remove the prunes from the liquid and transfer them to a small bowl to cool. Cut the prunes into halves or quarters.

3. Continue to simmer the cooking liquid very gently over low heat for 3 to 5 minutes or until it reaches a syruplike consistency. Pour the syrup into another small bowl or a pitcher to cool.

4. Cut the greens off the turnips, leaving a small decorative piece attached to each turnip.

5. In a large pot of boiling salted water, blanch the turnips for 10 to 15 minutes or until tender. Drain and immediately submerge in cold water to stop the cooking. Drain again.

6. Melt the butter in a small sauté pan over medium-high heat. When the butter is melted, add the turnips and sauté for 5 to 8 minutes or until nicely browned all over. Remove from the heat and cut each turnip lengthwise into quarters. Return to the pan and keep warm until ready to serve.

7. In a medium-sized bowl, whisk together the milk, egg, and cinnamon and a pinch of salt until blended. Pour into a shallow bowl or small gratin dish.

8. Lightly grease a large nonstick skillet or sauté pan and place over medium-high heat.

9. Dip both sides of 3 slices of the brioche into the milk mixture. Let them sit in the mixture for only a few seconds; do not let the mixture saturate the slices completely. Using a slotted spatula, transfer the soaked bread to the skillet and cook for 1 to 1½ minutes on each side or until golden. Transfer each piece of French toast to a small plate. Soak and cook the remaining brioche.

10. Garnish each serving of French toast with turnip quarters, prunes, and a drizzle of the brandy-prune syrup. Serve immediately.

fish and seafood
amuse

RAZOR CLAMS WITH CHARRED
CORN AND CORN PUREE

serves 6 to 10

I first tasted razor clams in Paris in 1991. I discovered them at an all-seafood restaurant—the first I had experienced—called Le Divellec, owned by Chef Jacques Divellec. Razor clams truly are great looking, although if you have never seen one, you might not even realize that a plump, tender clam dwells inside the textured, elongated shell, which rather resembles an old-fashioned straight razor. But the clam nestled inside tastes meaty rather than fishy and, like meat, slices easily. These clams, mainly available during a relatively short spring-into-early-summer season, are long and narrow with a protruding neck. Although they are found in both the Atlantic and Pacific oceans, they are more common along the Pacific coast. Keep an eye out for them. For this amuse, *you'll need six to ten clams, which, depending on their size, will together weigh about half a pound.*

I particularly like the long, beautiful, brown-and-yellow shells for presentation, which means this is a dish that easily impresses. Take care when handling the shells; they're sharp and delicate, and can easily crack. The charred corn marries happily with the clams and you will note that the cup of white wine needed for cooking the clams provides a fair amount of acid, which makes the flavor of the clams pop.

½ pound razor clams, rinsed in lightly salted water and scrubbed	1 bunch fresh thyme
Kosher or coarse salt	1½ cups fresh corn kernels (from 3 ears)
1 cup dry white wine	Salt and freshly ground black pepper
1 shallot, finely chopped	1 teaspoon olive oil

1. After rinsing and scrubbing the clams, lay them in a single layer on a tray or in a shallow dish. Handle the clams carefully; the shells are fragile and can easily crack. Sprinkle liberally with kosher or coarse salt and let them sit for about 15 minutes. Rinse and repeat. Rinse the clams very well before proceeding with the recipe. The salt draws the clams from their shells and in the process cleans them of sand and grit.

2. Put the clams in a medium-sized saucepan with the white wine, chopped shallot, and sprigs of thyme. Cover the pan and steam over high heat, shaking the pan occasionally, for about

5 minutes or until the clams become firm. These clams won't open like a normal clam, but the protruding meat will become firm and opaque. Remove from the heat. Remove the clams from the liquid (discard any that have not opened) and chill thoroughly. Discard the liquid.

3. To char the corn, heat a small heavy-bottomed sauté pan or cast-iron skillet over medium-high heat. When the pan is hot, add 1 cup of the corn kernels to the pan and cook, turning, until all the kernels are charred and cooked through. Remove the pan from the heat and spread the corn on a flat plate to cool.

4. In a medium-sized saucepan filled with boiling water, blanch the remaining ½ cup of corn kernels for 1 to 2 minutes or until tender. Drain the corn.

5. Combine the ½ cup blanched corn kernels with a small amount of water in a blender and puree. With the motor running, add as much additional water as necessary to form a sauce-like consistency. Season to taste with salt and pepper. Strain through a *chinois* or fine-mesh sieve into a small bowl.

6. Remove the clams from their shells, keeping the bottom shells and discarding the top shells. Using only the meat that protruded from the shells (the sand sacks in the shells can very easily get mixed up with the meat inside the shell, so be very careful), thinly slice the clams and toss with the olive oil to separate the slices. Season lightly with salt and pepper.

7. To serve, sprinkle some charred corn on a reserved shell. Arrange some of the sliced clams over the corn. Spoon a small amount of corn sauce over the slices and sprinkle with a few more kernels of charred corn. Repeat to make 5 to 9 more servings.

SOFT-SHELL CRABS WITH CUCUMBER ASPIC AND MARINATED CUCUMBER

serves 6

I have been known to rhapsodize about soft-shell crabs at Christmastime, when their spring season is still several cold months away. They definitely rank among my top ten favorite foods in the world and I look forward to them all year long! I love to pair cucumbers with sautéed crabs because of the crisp, clear, light flavors and textures of both.

Soft-shell crabs are blue crabs, which shed their hard shells as they grow out of them several times during the spring and summer. At this point, their new, growing shell is exceptionally soft and the crabs can be eaten whole, shell and all. The shell is at its softest only for six or seven hours, so the best soft-shell crabs are relatively rare. These crabs, called nonmolting soft-shell crabs, are what we use at Tru. They are harvested at the very beginning or very end of the cycle and are particularly plump and tender. Sautéed in a little olive oil, they are so sumptuous, they explode in your mouth with nutty flavor. Buy extra crabs to make sandwiches with the next day.

I serve this with cucumber aspic to perpetuate the lightness of the dish. Happily, aspics are experiencing a renaissance as we learn to make them with less gelatin so they're not rubbery. This one is light and refreshingly cold in the mouth. I am partial to cucumbers, and while I like all varieties, the early seedless English or European-style cukes are the best choice here.

3 soft-shell crabs (see Note)	¼ cup diced Cucumber Aspic
2 tablespoons olive oil	(page 250)
Salt and freshly ground black pepper	6 fresh chives, for garnishing
¼ cup Marinated Cucumber	
(recipe follows)	

1. If the soft-shell crabs are alive, clean them by first cutting behind the eyes to remove the eyes and the mouth. Fold back one side of the top shell, exposing the gills. Scrape off and discard the gills. Repeat with the other side of the shell. Flip the crab over onto its shell and fold back the tail (apron) section. Pull away and discard.

2. Heat the olive oil in a large sauté pan over medium-high heat. When the oil is hot, put the crabs in the pan, shell side down, and cook for about 3 minutes or until browned. Season to taste with salt and pepper. Turn the crabs over and cook for 2 to 3 minutes longer or until the undersides are browned and the crabs are cooked through. Season with salt and pepper. Remove the pan from the heat and transfer the crabs to a cutting board. Split each crab in half horizontally.

3. To serve, arrange half a crab on a small plate along with some of the marinated cucumber. Garnish the plate with diced cucumber aspic and a chive. Repeat to make 5 more servings.

NOTE: Always buy live soft-shell crabs. If you don't want to kill and clean them yourself, ask the fishmonger to do it for you. Store them in the refrigerator sitting on a damp towel and cover them with a damp towel. Cook them on the same day you buy them. In the restaurant, they come in large boxes lined with straw; the cool darkness and the moist straw keeps them alive.

MARINATED CUCUMBER

makes about 2 cups

1 large English cucumber, peeled, halved, and cut crosswise into thin slices	¼ cup rice wine vinegar ¼ teaspoon curry powder Salt and freshly ground black pepper

Put the cucumber slices in a glass or ceramic bowl. Toss with the vinegar and curry powder. Season to taste with salt and pepper. Cover and refrigerate for at least 1 hour. Serve chilled.

SMOKED SALMON PARFAIT
WITH CHIVE OIL

---

serves 6

This dish was devised out of necessity in our restaurant kitchen but will translate beautifully to yours. At Tru, I smoke and serve pounds and pounds of salmon every week, which means I end up with pounds of tasty scraps. I use the scraps to make this airy parfait, which for me exemplifies a small, light dish that bursts with flavor. It's also playful—the parfait can be cut into a variety of shapes, such as hearts for Valentine's Day or stars for the Fourth of July. Make this with small amounts of smoked salmon or, if you have them, smoked salmon scraps.

12 ounces smoked salmon	Chive Oil (recipe follows)
2½ cups heavy cream	1½ teaspoons wasabi *tobika* caviar,
½ cup cold water	or black caviar or salmon eggs,
7 sheets gelatin	for garnishing, optional
¼ teaspoon Champagne vinegar or	6 sprigs fresh chervil or flat-leaf
white wine vinegar	parsley, for garnishing
Salt	

1. Put the salmon and 1¼ cups of the cream in a large saucepan. Add the ½ cup water and bring to a simmer over medium-high heat. As soon as the mixture simmers, remove from the heat.

2. Meanwhile, fill a large bowl with cold water. Gently drop the gelatin sheets into the water, several at a time, until all are submerged. Let soften and bloom for about 5 minutes.

3. Transfer the salmon and its cooking liquid to a blender and puree. You will have to do this in batches. Strain each batch through a *chinois* or fine-mesh sieve into a medium-sized bowl.

4. Using your hands, lift the gelatin sheets from the water and squeeze them gently between your fingers. Transfer to the salmon puree and stir gently until dissolved. Stir in the vinegar and season to taste with salt. Allow to cool to room temperature.

5. Beat the remaining 1¼ cups heavy cream in a chilled small bowl with chilled beaters until stiff peaks form.

6. Fold the whipped cream into the salmon mixture a third at a time, working quickly before it sets.

7. Spoon into a lightly greased, shallow 9-by-7-inch pan. Smooth the surface. Cover with plastic wrap and refrigerate for at least 4 hours and up to 8 hours.

8. Using a small sharp knife or a cookie cutter, cut the parfait into shapes.

9. To serve, gently lift the shapes from the pan with a thin-bladed spatula. Put 1 or 2 of the shapes on a small plate and drizzle a little chive oil around them. Garnish each with a little caviar and a sprig of chervil. Repeat to make 5 more servings.

CHIVE OIL

makes about 4 cups

| 2 ½ cups grapeseed oil | 2 cups coarsely snipped fresh chives |

1. Heat ¼ cup of the oil in a skillet over high heat until almost smoking. Add the chives and cook for 1 minute or until wilted. Remove from the heat and allow to cool.

2. Scrape the chives and any oil into a blender. Add just enough of the remaining oil so that the chives will spin when the blender is turned on. Blend for about 5 minutes or until the oil is thick, smooth, and evenly green. Strain the oil through a *chinois* or fine-mesh sieve into a small bowl.

3. Transfer the chive oil to a glass container, cover, and refrigerate for up to 3 days. The oil will turn brown, but the off color does not mean it is bad.

SASHIMI OF FLUKE WITH
RADISH SALAD AND CHIVES

serves 6

Nobu, the Japanese restaurant in New York City's TriBeCa, is one of my favorite haunts, run by one of my favorite chefs. After eating fluke there one evening, I was inspired to develop this dish. Chef Nobu Matsuhisa does a hot sashimi presentation at the table by pouring boiling seasoned oil over fresh, raw fish. This flash-cooks the fish as it adds seasoning.

The radish salad is an outgrowth of my own curiosity. When I see two, three, or more varieties of a vegetable or fruit in the market, I buy them all and play around with them. Here, the different radishes add color, interest, and depth of flavor. The yuzu provides citrus zing, so integral to my cooking. You will find as you read through my recipes that I use citrus as a seasoning much like other chefs use salt and pepper. I keep a bowl filled with lemons, limes, oranges, and yuzu nearby at all times. Yuzu is a knobby, seed-filled Asian citrus fruit with an intense flavor somewhere between lemon and lime, but one that is still all its own. Try it; you'll love it as much as I do.

3 ounces sushi-quality fluke fillet	Salt and freshly ground black pepper
1 small black radish	1 teaspoon fresh *yuzu* juice or lime juice
1 red radish	
1 icicle radish	1 teaspoon grated lime zest
1 tablespoon rice wine vinegar	1 tablespoon finely snipped chives, for garnishing
1 tablespoon olive oil	

1. Clean the fillet of any remaining skin and bones. Slice the fish on the bias into 6 paper-thin slices and set aside.

2. Using a Japanese mandolin or a sharp knife, slice the radishes into paper-thin slices. Put the slices in a small bowl and toss with the vinegar and 1½ teaspoons of the oil. Season to taste with salt and pepper.

3. To serve, mound equal portions of the radish salad onto 6 small plates. Top each salad with a slice of fluke and, using a small pastry brush, lightly coat the fish with the remaining 1½ teaspoons olive oil and then the *yuzu*. Garnish each serving with a sprinkling of lime zest and chives.

PRINCE EDWARD ISLAND MUSSELS WITH RED CARROTS AND ORANGE-SAFFRON SAUCE

serves 6

I am one of those people who dream about lunch and dinner while eating breakfast, and I nearly always hope mussels will figure into one or the other. While you can use any fresh mussels for this summertime amuse, I like Prince Edward Island mussels because the waters surrounding that eastern Canadian island are clean and delightfully cool, not icy, which makes them the perfect environment for sweet, meaty mussels. Rinse and scrub the mussels gently and discard any that feel too light, which means they are only empty shells. Likewise, if the shells fall apart when you push gently on them, the mussels are dead. For this reason, buy extras; they're a bargain anyhow. Cook the mussels until they open, and discard those that don't open; too many people undercook mussels, so the mussels never plump up.

Although I have long loved steamed mussels with garlic and herbs, for this dish I serve them on a bed of steamed carrots with a creamy sauce infused with citrus and saffron. If you choose to serve this amuse in the mussel shells, be sure to scrub the shells well for a great presentation.

½ pound Prince Edward Island or other black or green mussels, rinsed and scrubbed	1 cup fresh orange juice
	½ cup heavy cream
	Salt and freshly ground black pepper
1 cup dry white wine	4 ounces baby carrots, scraped and
1 shallot, finely chopped	cut to be about 2 inches long,
1 bunch fresh thyme	if necessary
Pinch of saffron threads	¼ cup olive oil

1. Preheat a medium-sized saucepan until hot. Put the mussels in the hot saucepan with the white wine, chopped shallot, and sprigs of thyme. Cover and steam over high heat, shaking the pan occasionally, for 3 to 5 minutes or until the mussels have opened. Remove from the heat. Discard any unopened mussels. Remove the mussels from the liquid, allow to cool, and chill thoroughly. Discard all but ¼ cup of the liquid.

2. Put the reserved liquid, the saffron, and the orange juice in a medium-sized, heavy-bottomed saucepan. Bring to a boil over medium-high heat. Reduce the heat and simmer until the sauce has reduced to ¼ cup.

3. Add the heavy cream and bring to a boil. Immediately remove the pan from the heat.

4. Strain the sauce through a *chinois* or fine-mesh sieve into a small bowl. Season to taste with salt and pepper and allow to cool. Cover and chill.

5. Pour about 1 inch of water into a large saucepan and bring to a boil. Layer the carrots on a steamer rack and insert the rack in the pan, over the boiling water. Cover and steam for about 5 minutes or until the carrots are tender. Remove the carrots and allow to cool. Cut the carrots into thin slices along the diagonal, transfer to a medium-sized bowl, and toss with the oil. Season to taste with salt.

6. To serve, remove the mussels from their shells and discard the shells, or save 6 of the most perfect for serving. Make a bed of a few carrot slices on a small plate or mussel shell and top with a mussel. Drizzle orange-saffron sauce over the mussel. Repeat to make 5 more servings.

MINI LOBSTER CLUB SANDWICH
WITH TAHITIAN VANILLA BEAN AIOLI

serves 6

When I worked in England in the early 1980s, I took advantage of my six-week vacations to work at other European restaurants. This led to a stage at Michel Guerard's famous restaurant in Eugénie-les-Bains, France. I was fascinated by his wood-burning oven that was, in some ways, more of an open fireplace. Before sending them out the door to the dining room, the chef cooked half lobsters on racks over the fire, basting them with vanilla butter and then sprinkling them with fresh herbs from his kitchen garden. So simple, smoky, and buttery!

At Tru, I was compelled to play with those evocative flavors for an amuse, *making a vanilla bean aioli and serving the lobster with pancetta in a "mini club sandwich." Cook a single 1½-pound lobster and use the tail or claw meat, or buy cooked lobster meat. You don't need much for an* amuse. *Everyone loves these cute little bites.*

3 slices pancetta, each about ⅛ inch thick	½ cup mizuna leaves or other tender greens
Six ¼-inch-thick slices bread, cut from a baguette	3 ounces cooked lobster meat, from the tail or claw of a 1½- to
2 tablespoons Tahitian Vanilla Bean Aioli (recipe follows)	2-pound lobster (see Note)
	Salt and freshly ground black pepper

1. Preheat the oven to 325°F.
2. Arrange the pancetta slices in a single layer on a rimmed baking sheet. Bake for 10 to 15 minutes or until crisp. Cut the slices in half and transfer to a flat plate. Keep at room temperature until ready to use.
3. Toast one side of each piece of bread under the broiler until golden brown.
4. To serve, spread the untoasted side of each slice of bread with 1 teaspoon of the aioli and place on a small plate. Arrange some mizuna leaves over the aioli and top with a pancetta half. Divide the lobster into 6 portions and season to taste with salt and pepper. Top off each sandwich with a portion of the lobster.

NOTE: Buy cooked lobster meat from a reputable fishmonger, or if cooking it yourself, be sure to buy living, lively lobsters. If you can, hold the lobster behind its claws and check that it snaps its tail tightly under its body—this signals a healthy crustacean. It's best to buy lobsters from a fishmonger with good turnover. Once in captivity, lobsters are not fed and as time passes, their flesh shrinks from the shells. Recently trapped lobsters have the plumpest, sweetest meat. If you can, buy them right off the boat from a Maine lobsterman— or you can mail-order these "day-boat lobsters" and have them sent by overnight air (see page 253). Keep lobsters alive by storing them in the refrigerator until ready to use. Cook them on the day you buy them.

Bring a pot of lightly salted water to a boil over high heat. One lobster needs at least 1 gallon of water for quick cooking. Drop the lobster headfirst into the boiling water. When the water returns to a boil, reduce the heat and simmer gently until the lobster turns bright red. The rule of thumb is 8 minutes per pound, with 2 minutes added for every ¼ pound. A 1½-pound lobster will need about 12 minutes. Lift the cooked lobster from the water with tongs and set aside to cool.

When cool, hold the lobster over the sink to let any excess water drain. Twist the claws from the body and use a pick or small fork to pull out the luscious meat. Use a knife or your hands to separate the tail from the body. Pull the tail meat from the shell with a pick or small fork. Cooked lobster meat can be refrigerated for up to 24 hours.

TAHITIAN VANILLA BEAN AIOLI

makes about 1 cup

1 large egg	1 Tahitian vanilla bean, split
1 large egg yolk	lengthwise and seeds scraped
2 tablespoons fresh lemon juice	(see Note)
¼ teaspoon Dijon mustard	1 cup olive oil
1 teaspoon salt	

1. Put the egg, egg yolk, lemon juice, mustard, salt, and vanilla bean seeds in a food processor or blender. Process for about 30 seconds or until well combined. With the motor running, add the oil in a slow, steady stream and process until all the oil has been emulsified and the mayonnaise is thick and smooth.

2. Transfer to a glass or ceramic bowl, cover, and refrigerate until ready to use. The aioli keeps for up to 3 days.

NOTE: After you use the vanilla bean, store the pod buried in sugar to make vanilla sugar (great in coffee!) or toss it in canola, grapeseed, or light olive oil and use it to flavor vinaigrette for seafood salad or grilled fish. The pod still has a lot of flavor.

POTATO-AND-BASIL-WRAPPED
TUNA ROLL

serves 6

This amuse, *so fun and contemporary, is also a great hors d'oeuvre, delicious if dipped in a little soy sauce mixed with wasabi or with an aioli. I like to pass the sliced logs on a mirrored tray for a spectacular presentation. As an* amuse, *I serve it with drizzles of pesto oil.*

You will need a mandolin or potato-slicing wheel to cut the potato into very thin strips that can be wrapped around the tuna without cracking. The quick frying crisps the potato but leaves the tuna raw—for "potato sushi," rather than rice sushi—and conveys sensual experiences of hot and cold, brittle and tender. Use top-grade yellow fin or blue fin tuna, which is so fresh, it's called sushi quality. Once you wrap the tuna in the sliced potatoes, don't wait to deep-fry them, or the potatoes will brown and dry out.

1 pound sushi-quality tuna	Vegetable oil
1 tablespoon extra-virgin olive oil	Pesto Oil (page 246)
Salt and freshly ground black pepper	Black and white sesame seeds
8 to 10 large fresh basil leaves	Microgreens or fresh sprigs chervil,
1 Red Bliss or russet potato	for garnishing

1. Cut the tuna into 2 logs, making them as squared and even as possible. Each should be about 1 inch thick. Brush with the olive oil and season to taste with salt and pepper.

2. Wrap the tuna logs with the basil leaves, pressing the leaves into the sides of the fish so that they cling to the oil. Position them so that they enclose the tuna logs, with just the ends exposed.

3. Using a Japanese mandolin or a turning vegetable slicer, slice the potatoes into long, thin strips. Drop the strips into water to prevent them from browning.

4. Wrap the longest strips around the tuna logs to cover the basil leaves. Let the strips overlap slightly.

5. Pour vegetable oil into a deep, heavy saucepan to a depth of 3 inches, or enough oil to cover each log completely when it is lowered into it. Heat over high heat until a deep-frying thermometer registers 425°F.

6.   Using tongs, gently and carefully submerge one of the logs in the hot oil and fry for about 10 seconds or until the potatoes are golden brown. Lift from the oil with the tongs, taking care not to crack the coating. Set aside on paper towels to cool. Repeat with the other log.

7.   To serve, season the logs with more salt and pepper, and slice into twelve ¼-inch slices. Put 2 pieces on each of 6 small plates and drizzle with a little pesto oil. Sprinkle the rolls lightly with sesame seeds and garnish with a few sprigs of microgreens.

AVOCADO-PEEKYTOE CRAB SALAD BALL WITH CITRUS VINAIGRETTE

serves 6

It's not easy to make luscious, velvety avocados look elegant, so for this rich-tasting amuse I formed the avocado into spheres by molding it inside small squares of plastic wrap. Inside each avocado sphere is a colorful and intriguing mixture of sweet crabmeat, ripe, juicy mango, red onion, bell pepper, and cucumber. The amuse is served with a drizzle of citrus vinaigrette, which makes the flavors sing like a well-rehearsed choir.

Peekytoe crabs are blue crabs harvested from the clear, cold waters off the coast of central Maine. They're especially sweet, moist, and tender, but you can use any good, fresh crabmeat, such as that of the Jonah crab. The best Jonah crabs, close relatives of rock crabs, are sweet and succulent. It's their leg meat that's prized, while the Peekytoe and other blue crabs are esteemed for their body and leg meat.

6 ounces cooked Peekytoe or Jonah crabmeat, or other high-quality crabmeat	2 tablespoons honey
	2 tablespoons fresh lemon juice
	2 tablespoons fresh lime juice
1 tablespoon finely minced red bell pepper	Salt and freshly ground black pepper
	3 ripe avocados
1 tablespoon finely minced red onion	2 to 3 tablespoons Citrus Vinaigrette (page 244)
1 tablespoon finely minced cucumber	
1 tablespoon finely minced ripe mango	

1. Pick through the crabmeat to remove any bits of shell. Transfer to a glass or ceramic bowl, cover, and refrigerate until needed.

2. Toss the pepper, onion, cucumber, and mango with the crabmeat.

3. In a small bowl, whisk together the honey, lemon juice, and lime juice. Add to the crab mixture and toss gently. Season to taste with salt and pepper.

4. Peel the avocados. Cut each one in half and remove and discard the pit. With a sharp knife, square off each avocado half and thinly slice crosswise.

5.   Cut out six 5-inch squares of plastic wrap. Fan 4 slices of avocado in the center of each square of plastic wrap so that the pieces of avocado overlap slightly. Center a small mound of the crabmeat mixture on the avocado slices. Bring the corners of the plastic wrap together and twist, forming a ball of crabmeat completely enclosed in avocado. Repeat to make 5 more balls. Chill until ready to serve.

6.   To serve, unwrap the avocado-crabmeat balls and put each one on a small serving plate. Garnish each with a drizzle of citrus vinaigrette.

Caviar has to be the ultimate amuse. *Just a small bite satisfies the palate yet leaves you yearning for another taste. I've loved it from first bite, and so when Gale Gand, my culinary partner, and I opened Trio in Evanston, Illinios, in the early 1990s, I wanted caviar to be a signature dish. When my customers thought of caviar, I wanted them to think of me. I wanted the experience of eating caviar to leave a positive and personal impression.*

On the day we opened Trio, I took a walk along the streets of downtown Evanston to clear my head and escape the intensity and craziness at the restaurant. I was frustrated because I had not yet come up with a dramatic way to serve caviar. As I passed an art-supply store, an artist's palette caught my eye. "That's it!" I thought. "I will serve the caviar and its garnishes on a palette, arranged like painter's paints." I bought two dozen acrylic palettes and rushed back to Trio. Who would have thought these would significantly change my life? The caviar palette was a huge hit, but when I left Trio, I left it behind.

When it was time to open Tru five years later, I was eager to re-create a new vision for caviar. Seeking to literally elevate the caviar, I came up with the idea of a staircase. Howard Harris, who was working with me designing glass butter plates and face plates, accepted the challenge of fabricating my design for a spiral staircase for the caviar. It took several months of trial and error, but in the end we had this magnificent glass staircase. It was my idea to etch my signature in the staircase as a play on the concept of a signature dish. Today, about 95 percent of our customers order the caviar staircase, which means the restaurant's fifty staircases are in constant use. (For information on ordering one, see page 255.)

True caviar is the roe of three types of sturgeon that swim in the Caspian Sea: beluga, osetra, and sevruga. Iran borders on the southern coast of the Caspian Sea and is known for harvesting and selling the best caviar in the world, which is why we try to use Iranian caviar exclusively. I like other caviar, but I revere Iranian caviar. Sure, it's expensive, but you need so little for an amuse, *it's easy to stay within your budget. And if you've never tried caviar, this is a great way to do so.*

The big, gray to ink-black grains of beluga caviar are considered the finest in the world. Osetra, with its vaguely nutty flavor and smaller grains, is preferred by some, while still others like sevruga's bolder taste—and slightly lower price tag. All are magnificent. The type of caviar depends on the size of the sturgeon when it's harvested. Caspian Sea sturgeon are so good because of the optimal conditions in those waters. Farmed American and

Chinese sturgeon produce admirable caviar too. Roe from salmon, whitefish, lumpfish, and trout are also marketed as "caviar" but, while tasty, are not the real deal.

When you buy caviar, buy it from a reputable dealer. Make sure it's been stored in a cold place where the temperature hovers around the freezing mark. The eggs should be whole and full and should smell pleasingly of the sea when the tin is opened.

Store unopened tins or jars of caviar in the coldest part of the refrigerator, pushed to the back of the box. They keep for about three weeks, but once opened, should be consumed within forty-eight hours. I have never found this to be a problem.

I am not supplying a recipe for this dish. Look at the picture and decide how you would like to serve caviar as an amuse. Here, I use just a teaspoonful of different kinds and serve them on crisp toasts garnished with a selection of minced red onion, chopped hard-cooked egg yolks and whites, capers, and a little crème fraîche, homemade (page 252) or store-bought. These are the caviars I use most often: beluga caviar, Iranian Karaburun caviar, sevruga caviar, salmon caviar, smoked whitefish caviar, wasabi tobiko, golden caviar.

FROG LEG TERRINE WITH SHERRY VINAIGRETTE, WALNUTS, FRISÉE, AND CHERRY TOMATOES

serves 6 to 10

You've probably heard that frogs' legs taste like chicken. It's true. As a child, I contentedly ate them whenever my grandmother cooked them—floured, dipped in eggs, sautéed, and then served with a spicy tomato sauce. I always liked them that way, but the first time I tasted plump, lean frogs' legs sautéed with garlic and herbs, I knew I was tasting something remarkable. For this reason, I categorize frogs' legs with escargot and French onion soup: You can't believe how good they are until you try them. I'm indebted to Chef Nico Lidenis of Nico's restaurant in London, who taught me a lot of great ways to serve frogs' legs when I did a stage there.

For this amuse, I make a terrine from the meat of the frogs' legs, gently flavored with butter, garlic, white wine, and parsley. I serve it with a light sherry vinaigrette sprinkled over crunchy frisée and garnished with walnuts.

It's not unusual to find frogs' legs in a supermarket, and surely a good fish merchant can get them for you. Like chicken, they freeze well, so if you think you might want to try this, buy the frogs' legs when you see them and stow them in the freezer.

10 to 12 pairs frogs' legs, about 1 pound	2 tablespoons finely chopped fresh parsley
2 tablespoons unsalted butter	4 ounces walnuts
6 tablespoons dry white wine	6 tablespoons sherry wine vinegar
1½ cups water	2 tablespoons extra-virgin olive oil
Salt and freshly ground black pepper	6 to 10 cherry tomatoes
1 tablespoon finely minced garlic	Frisée lettuce, for garnishing
Nonstick cooking spray	

1. Rinse the frogs' legs. Split each pair of legs through the joint. Remove the meat from the bones and reserve the meat and bones separately.

2. Heat 1 tablespoon of the butter in a medium-sized sauté pan or skillet over medium heat.

When the butter is hot, add the leg bones and sauté for 6 to 8 minutes or until golden brown.

3. Pour off the butter and add the wine to the pan. Increase the heat and bring to a boil while scraping the bottom of the pan with a wooden spoon. Add the water and reduce the heat to a simmer. Simmer over very low heat for about 15 minutes or until reduced by half.

4. Remove from the heat and strain the contents of the pan through a *chinois* or fine-mesh sieve into a shallow bowl. Discard the bones. Season the broth to taste with salt and pepper and set aside to cool to room temperature.

5. Wipe out the sauté pan and add the remaining 1 tablespoon butter. Melt over medium-low heat. Add the reserved meat and garlic and cook gently for about 5 minutes or until the meat is cooked through and tender.

6. Remove from the heat and put the meat in a medium-sized bowl. Season to taste with salt and pepper and set aside to cool to room temperature.

7. Lightly coat a long, shallow, 1-cup terrine mold, approximately 3 inches long and 2 inches wide, with nonstick cooking spray and line with plastic wrap, leaving 3-inch overhangs on the long sides of the terrine.

8. Remove any fat from the surface of the broth and discard. Add the broth and parsley to the leg meat and mix well. Transfer the mixture to the prepared terrine.

9. Place the mold on a rimmed tray to catch any overflow of juices. Fold the overhanging ends of the plastic wrap over the top of the terrine and set a piece of foil-lined lightweight cardboard, cut to fit inside the mold, on top of the plastic wrap. Place a weight, such as a soup can laid on its side, on top of the cardboard and refrigerate for at least 8 hours.

10. Preheat the oven to 350°F.

11. Spread the nuts in a single layer on a baking sheet or in a jelly-roll pan and toast for about 10 minutes or until the nuts are lightly browned and fragrant. Shake the pan 2 or 3 times while the nuts are toasting. Transfer the nuts to a plate to cool to room temperature. Chop them coarsely. Store in a covered container until ready to use.

12. Put the sherry wine vinegar in a small bowl and whisk in the olive oil until blended. Season to taste with salt and pepper.

13. To serve, use the plastic wrap to lift the terrine from the mold. Unwrap and cut the terrine into ¼-inch slices. Place the slices on a work surface and use a small cookie cutter to trim the slices into perfect rounds. Lay 1 round on a small plate and garnish with toasted walnuts, cherry tomatoes, and frisée lettuce. Drizzle with some sherry vinaigrette. Repeat to make 5 to 9 more servings.

TOWER OF FINGERLING POTATO
WITH BELUGA CAVIAR

serves 6

This is an elegant one-bite amuse guaranteed to wow your guests and get their palates going for the meal to come. I recommend fingerling potatoes because they are tiny and buttery, but you could slice and fry another small all-purpose potato instead. Although you can buy it at a specialty store or cheese shop, I like to make my own crème fraîche. And, please, if you can, use beluga caviar, the best Iranian caviar available. It's expensive, but you need only an ounce—so don't be cheap about it!

¼ cup crème fraîche, homemade (page 252) or store-bought	Vegetable oil
1 tablespoon fresh lemon juice	1 to 2 fingerling potatoes, unpeeled
Salt and freshly ground black pepper	1 ounce beluga caviar

1. In a small bowl, whisk together the crème fraîche and lemon juice until blended. Season to taste with salt and pepper, cover, and refrigerate until ready to use.

2. Pour the vegetable oil into a deep, heavy saucepan to a depth of 2 inches. Heat over high heat until a deep-frying thermometer registers 350°F.

3. Meanwhile, use a Japanese mandolin to cut the potato crosswise into 18 very thin slices. If you don't have a mandolin, use a small sharp knife to cut very thin slices.

4. Gently pat the potato slices with paper towels. Drop the slices into the hot oil and fry for 1 to 2 minutes or until golden brown. Remove from the oil with a slotted spoon or spider and drain on a double thickness of paper towels. Sprinkle with salt while still hot. Transfer the chips to a wire rack to cool.

5. To serve, place a small dollop of the crème fraîche mixture on 3 of the chips. Stack the chips, with the crème fraîche facing up, on a small plate. Top with caviar. Repeat to make 5 more servings.

AHI TUNA CUBE WITH TOASTED BLACK AND WHITE SESAME SEEDS

serves 6

As successful as this is as an amuse, *it is an equally amazing hors d'oeuvre. I came up with this recipe one day when we were fooling around with cubed Cheddar cheese and trying to imagine what other foods would cut neatly into cubes. One of my cooks, Jason Wheeler, suggested tuna and all of a sudden our fun morphed into an outstanding* amuse. *The cubes of raw tuna look contemporary on the plate and the toasted sesame seeds enhance their flavor. Like cheese cubes, you could serve a whole tray of these at your next party, lined up geometrically and pierced with fancy toothpicks or cool-looking olive swords.*

1 tablespoon mixed black and white sesame seeds	2 tablespoons organic soy sauce
	3 tablespoons sesame oil
3 ounces ahi or bluefin tuna or other sushi-quality tuna steak	

1. Put the sesame seeds in a dry frying pan and toast over medium heat for about 30 seconds or until fragrant and the white seeds start to turn golden. Transfer to a small, shallow bowl and allow to cool completely.

2. Cut the tuna into six ½-inch cubes.

3. To serve, coat one side of each cube with the sesame seeds and place on a small plate with the coated side facing up. Drizzle soy sauce and sesame oil over the cubes.

KUMAMOTO OYSTERS WITH BLOOD ORANGE ASPIC

serves 4

For this clean-tasting amuse, *I chose Kumamoto oysters, the tiny Japanese bivalves that grow all along the Pacific coast of the United States. If you can't find them, substitute farm-raised Belons or bluepoints instead. The key is to find the juiciest, plumpest, butteriest, and freshest small oysters available. Chill them over crushed ice and don't wait long to eat them. I originally made a blood orange–juice vinaigrette for oysters, but when I garnished them with diced blood orange aspic, the dice resembled shining rubies. No pearls for these oysters!*

4 Kumamoto oysters, rinsed and scrubbed	3 to 4 tablespoons diced Blood Orange Aspic (recipe follows) Snipped fresh chives, for garnishing

1. Using an oyster knife, shuck the oysters. Remove and discard the top shells. Chill the oysters still nestled in the bottom shells. To do so, set them on a tray lined with rock salt or crushed ice and refrigerate until cold.

2. To serve, place an oyster on a small plate. Spoon diced aspic into the shell around the oyster and top with a snip of fresh chive. Repeat to make 3 more servings.

BLOOD ORANGE ASPIC

makes 1 thin layer in a 9-by-12-inch jelly-roll pan

5 to 6 blood oranges	9 sheets gelatin

1. Squeeze the juice from the oranges to measure about 2 cups of juice.

2. Strain the orange juice through a *chinois* or fine-mesh sieve into a medium-sized saucepan and bring to a simmer over medium-high heat. As soon as the juice simmers, remove from the heat.

3. Meanwhile, fill a large bowl with cold water. Gently drop the gelatin sheets into the water, several at a time, until all are submerged. Let soften and bloom for about 5 minutes.

4. Using your hands, lift the gelatin sheets from the water and squeeze them gently between your fingers. Transfer the sheets to the lukewarm juice. Stir gently until dissolved. Let cool at room temperature.

5. Pour the juice into a small jelly-roll pan, or other rimmed metal pan measuring about 9 by 12 inches, and allow to cool at room temperature. Refrigerate, uncovered, for about 4 hours or until set. When the jelly is set, cover with plastic wrap and refrigerate until needed.

LOBSTER-MANGO SPRING ROLL
WITH APRICOT VINAIGRETTE

serves 12; makes 4 rolls

I love this easy amuse *because losbter is always a crowd pleaser. This has Asian flair and it's not difficult to find rice paper wrappers. When you fill them with firm lobster meat mixed with crunchy cucumber and sweet mango, a simple spring roll transforms into a luxurious dish. The apricot vinaigrette is the perfect accent for this. You need only a little lobster, but even a little makes any dish special.*

1 cooked lobster tail from a 1½- to 2-pound lobster (see Note on page 95)	Four 6- to 8-inch round dried rice paper sheets (*banh trang*)
½ cucumber, peeled	Salt and freshly ground black pepper
1 ripe mango	3 to 4 tablespoons Apricot Vinaigrette (recipe follows)

1. Remove the lobster meat from the shell in one piece and cut the meat lengthwise into quarters. Trim each piece so that it is about 4 inches long. Pull out the digestive tract if it's present.

2. Remove the seeds from the cucumber with a small spoon or the small end of a melon baller. Discard the seeds. Cut 4 strips from the cucumber, each one about ⅓ inch thick and 4 inches long, so that they match the lobster strips. Make the strips as even as possible. Save any extra cucumber for another use.

3. Peel the skin from the mango with a vegetable peeler for easy removal. Slice the flesh to the pit, squaring it as much as you can. Cut 4 strips from the mango to match the cucumber strips. Make the strips as even as possible. Save any extra mango flesh for another use.

4. Fill a large, shallow bowl with warm water and spread a lint-free dish towel on a work surface.

5. One at a time, drop the rice paper sheets into the water until all are submerged. Soak for 3 minutes or until they are completely softened and pliable. Lift the sheets out of the water with your hands and spread them out on the dish towel to drain, making sure they don't overlap.

6.   Working with 1 wrapper at a time, arrange a strip each of lobster, cucumber, and mango across the bottom third of the wrapper. Season to taste with salt and pepper. Fold the wrapper over the filling and roll into a tight cylinder up to the halfway mark. Fold in the two sides and continue to roll until sealed. Place the roll on a flat plate, seam side down. Repeat to make 3 more rolls. Allow to rest for a few minutes to seal completely.

7.   To serve, cut the rolls on the bias into thirds. Spoon some vinaigrette on a small plate and set a slice on top of the sauce, cut side down. Or, slice the spring rolls into smaller pieces and serve on small plates with small ramekins of vinaigrette for dipping.

APRICOT VINAIGRETTE

makes about 3 cups

2 cups coarsely chopped dried apricots	¼ cup Simple Syrup (page 251)
	1 cup water
¾ cup rice wine vinegar	Salt

1.   Put the apricots in a small bowl and pour hot water over them. Let them soften for about 30 minutes. Drain and discard the soaking liquid.

2.   In a blender, combine the drained apricots, vinegar, and simple syrup and pulse to make a coarse puree.

3.   With the motor running, slowly add as much of the water as necessary for a fluid, smooth consistency. Season to taste with salt. Strain through a *chinoise* or fine-mesh sieve set over a small bowl. Transfer to a nonreactive covered container and refrigerate until needed. The vinaigrette will keep for up to 4 days.

SMOKED SALMON CREPES
WITH CREAM CHEESE

serves 6

I was blessed to work a stage at the legendary chef Alain Chapel's restaurant in France during the eighties and I will never forget him. Needless to say, the chef's influence on how I think about food and how I cook was significant. His overall brilliance had great impact on the culinary community and is still greatly missed. He made a dish similar to this one with smoked sturgeon, and so, in appreciation of what he taught me, I devised this pretty, yet simple, amuse. Layer the crepes and salmon as many times as you can—sandwiching them with cream cheese or crème fraîche—and then cut them into tiny wedges.

This resembles a savory napoleon, and I serve it with a simple garnish of celery leaves dressed with lemon and olive oil. Crepes are endlessly versatile and can be served with savory fillings, as here, or with sweet ones. They are somewhat out of style these days, and while they are destined to make a comeback (and it won't be their first), they are always welcome at Tru. Cook them in a crepe pan and make sure the flame is medium. If it's too high, the batter will toughen before it cooks, and the crepes will brown more than you want for this recipe.

2 ounces cream cheese, softened, or	5 Crepes (recipe follows)
¼ cup crème fraîche, homemade	½ cup celery leaves
(page 252) or store-bought	1 tablespoon olive oil
1 tablespoon fresh lemon juice	Grated zest of 1 lemon
Salt and freshly ground black pepper	1 teaspoon finely snipped chives
½ pound thinly sliced smoked	6 cucumber flowers, for garnishing
salmon	

1. Put the cream cheese in a small bowl with 2 teaspoons of the lemon juice. Mix well and season to taste with salt and pepper.

2. Using a 3-inch round cookie cutter, stamp out 4 rounds of smoked salmon and 5 rounds of crepes.

3. Place 1 crepe on a work surface and top with a salmon round. Spread about 1 tablespoon of

the cream cheese over the salmon. Continue the layering, so that you end with a plain crepe on top of the stack.

4. Put the celery leaves in a small bowl and toss with the olive oil, lemon zest, chives, and remaining 1 teaspoon lemon juice. Season to taste with salt and pepper.

5. To serve, divide the celery salad among 6 small plates. Cut the stack of salmon crepes into 6 wedges. Arrange a wedge and a cucumber flower on each plate.

CREPES

makes about 1½ cups; about 6 crepes

³/₄ cup all-purpose flour	1¼ cups milk
3 teaspoons sugar	3 large eggs
Pinch of salt	Melted butter

1. Whisk together the flour, sugar, and salt in a medium-sized bowl. Make a well in the center and pour in the milk. Whisk the milk into the flour mixture until the batter is smooth and well blended. Whisk in the eggs until blended.

2. Strain the batter through a sieve into another medium-sized bowl. Cover with plastic wrap and refrigerate for at least 2 hours to give the batter time to rest.

3. Heat an 8-inch nonstick skillet or crepe pan over medium heat. Lightly brush the pan with melted butter.

4. Ladle about ¼ cup of the batter into the skillet and tilt the pan in all directions to evenly coat the bottom. Cook the crepe for about 30 seconds or until the bottom is light brown. Loosen the edges with a spatula and flip the crepe over with the spatula or your fingers. Cook the underside for 10 to 15 seconds or until it is set, dry, and browned in spots. Slide the crepe onto a flat plate and cover with a piece of wax paper.

5. Repeat with the remaining batter, brushing the pan with more butter as needed, and stacking the crepes between wax paper. The crepes may be made up to 3 days ahead. Cover with plastic wrap and refrigerate. Bring to room temperature before using.

serves 6

Dungeness crab is the quintessential California seafood, although the crabs are harvested from Mexico to Alaska. I first tasted it about ten years ago, when chef-owner Michael Chiarello from Tra Vigne restaurant in St. Helena, California (one of my favorite restaurants in the world), cooked a whole crab in a wood-burning oven. It was so smoky, juicy, and just plain delicious, I decided to create an amuse that mimicked the smokiness of that dish with charred peppers. Dungeness crab is nearly always sold already cooked—unless you're lucky enough to buy it fresh off a boat on the West Coast. Then you'll have to cook it yourself.

½ pound cooked Dungeness crab
meat

¼ cup minced celery

2 tablespoons mayonnaise

Salt and freshly ground black pepper

2 yellow bell peppers

2 red bell peppers

½ cup pitted and chopped Picholine
olives, plus 1 to 2 tablespoons for
garnishing

½ cup water, plus more as needed

½ cup olive oil

Celery leaves, for garnishing

1. Pick through the crabmeat to remove any bits of shell. Put the meat in a medium-sized bowl.

2. Gently stir the celery and mayonnaise into the crabmeat and season to taste with salt and pepper. Cover and chill until ready to use.

3. Lightly char the peppers over a grill or gas flame, or under a broiler, until blackened on all sides and soft. When cool enough to handle, remove and discard the skins, ribs, and seeds. Coarsely chop the peppers. Reserve a small amount of diced peppers for garnishing.

4. Transfer the yellow peppers to a blender. Add a little water if necessary, and puree until smooth. Scrape the puree from the blender into a small bowl.

5. Transfer the red peppers to the blender. Add a little water if necessary, and puree until smooth. Scrape the puree from the blender into a small bowl.

6. Combine the olives and the ½ cup water in the blender and puree until the mixture is fluid. Slowly pour in the oil and puree until emulsified. Transfer the olive puree to a small bowl.

7. To serve, use 2 small spoons to form the crabmeat into oval-shaped quenelles. Put a quenelle on a small plate, then spoon some of the pepper and olive purees around the plate. Garnish with the reserved diced peppers, a celery leaf, and some chopped olives. Repeat to make 5 more servings.

CITRUS-MARINATED BAY SCALLOPS
WITH PETITE HERB SALAD

serves 6

Bay scallops are delicately sweet and very small—usually less than an inch thick and about half as wide. They are available from late fall to late winter and, while they tend to be expensive, are well worth buying. For this seviche-like amuse, *you need only three ounces, but the scallops must be superfresh. Thinly sliced, briefly marinated in a lovely citrus vinaigrette, they taste magnificent with a soft herb salad hit with a dash of the citrus dressing.*

Scallops harvested in American waters are shucked soon after they are caught, which is why it's unusual to find them in their pretty scalloped shells. Select pale-pinkish or -orangey bay scallops; if you're buying sea scallops, they should be creamy white or tinged with pink. No scallops should be bright white, which indicates they were soaked in a solution to extend their shelf life. (While this is not dangerous, it causes the mollusks to absorb water, which they will expel when marinated or cooked.) For this recipe, seek out the recommended bay scallops and marinate them on the day you buy them if at all possible.

2 tablespoons olive oil	3 ounces sushi-quality bay scallops
2 teaspoons fresh lemon juice	$\frac{1}{4}$ cup frisée microgreens
2 teaspoons fresh orange juice	$\frac{1}{4}$ cup fresh chervil leaves
2 teaspoons fresh lime juice	Salt and freshly ground black pepper

1. In a small bowl, whisk the olive oil with the lemon, orange, and lime juices.
2. Slice the scallops thinly and put in a small nonreactive bowl. Spoon half of the citrus dressing over the scallops and toss to mix.
3. Put the frisée and chervil in another small bowl and toss with as much of the remaining dressing as needed to coat the greens. Season to taste with salt and pepper.
4. To serve, drain the scallops. Put equal portions of the scallops onto 6 small plates. Season to taste with salt. Place a small amount of the salad alongside the scallops.

COD BRANDADE WITH
KALAMATA OLIVE CROSTINI

serves 6 to 10

When I was in Spain a few years ago, I was dazzled by the pure white marble tables set up in the Barcelona food markets to sell fresh and dried cod. The fresh fish was displayed in big water-filled tubs and the dried was packed in salt. I was equally impressed by the endless and creative ways Spanish cooks prepared salt cod, which we in America tend to dismiss as not very interesting. We're wrong. Dried cod has to be soaked for twenty-four hours in cold water and then milk to keep it white and creamy, but once it's hydrated, it's delicious. Here, I make it into a creamy brandade that is spooned onto crostini smeared with a simple olive and caper paste. The contrast of the creamy cod brandade and the bold-flavored olive paste makes a powerful amuse. This dish was inspired by the cooking of Martin Berasategie, who is the chef-owner of the three-star Michelin restaurant of the same name in Lasarte, Spain—and who also has his own line of china. Look for it; you'll love it!

½ pound salt cod (about 1 small side)	⅓ cup chopped flat-leaf parsley
Milk	½ cup pitted Kalamata olives
½ cup olive oil	2 tablespoons drained capers
½ cup heavy cream	1 clove garlic, chopped
Salt and freshly ground black pepper	6 to 10 slices baguette

1. Put the cod in a large ceramic or glass bowl and cover with cold water. (It may be necessary to slice the fish into sections to fit in the bowl.) Refrigerate for 24 hours, pouring off and replacing the water twice during soaking. During the final 8 hours, soak the fish in milk to cover. This keeps the fish white and gives it a clean, creamy flavor.

2. Remove the cod from the refrigerator and pour off the milk. Pull off and discard any skin and bones from the cod. Cut the flesh into 2-inch pieces.

3. Heat ¼ cup of the olive oil in a large sauté pan over low heat. When the oil is hot, add the cod. Cook for about 3 minutes on each side or until the cod is cooked through and the thickest part of the fish flakes easily.

4. Remove the pan from the heat and transfer the cod to a saucepan. Set the pan over medium heat and gradually pour in the cream and the remaining ¼ cup olive oil, working the mixture quickly and vigorously with a wooden spoon until the fish is reduced to a coarse puree and most of the liquid is absorbed. Season to taste with salt and pepper. Allow to cool, cover, and refrigerate.

5. When the cod *brandade* is cold, mix in the parsley.

6. Combine the olives, capers, and garlic in a blender and puree to a smooth paste. Transfer to a small bowl.

7. To serve, spread a thin layer of the olive paste over a slice of baguette. Top with a dollop of cod *brandade* and place on a small plate. Repeat to make 5 to 9 more servings.

BRAISED MANILA CLAMS WITH
SAUSAGE AND WHITE BEANS

serves 6 to 10

Who doesn't love New England clam chowder? This amuse *grabs the flavors of the chowder—chewy clams, crispy bacon, crunchy celery—and reconstructs them into a one-bite starter that, while not soup, will transport you directly to Cape Cod. I choose to use Pacific Ocean—grown Manila clams rather than littleneck clams, the smallest of the hard-shell Atlantic clams known as quahogs. Feel free to use littlenecks or the slightly larger cherrystones if you can't get tasty, tiny Manilas. Regardless of which clams you use, make sure their shells are tightly closed and they feel heavy and full of juice when you buy them, and soak and rinse them in cold water two or three times to remove all sand and grit. Always buy clams from a reputable market with good turnover.*

1 cup dried white beans	1 shallot, finely chopped
3 fresh sage leaves	1 bunch fresh thyme
¼ pound sweet Italian sausage	Salt and freshly ground black pepper
½ pound Manila clams, rinsed and scrubbed	¼ cup extra-virgin olive oil
1 cup dry white wine	Chopped flat-leaf parsley, for garnishing

1. In a large bowl, combine the beans with enough cold water to cover by 2 inches. Soak the beans for at least 6 hours. Drain and transfer to a large saucepan or a stockpot.

2. Add enough cold water to cover the beans by 3 inches. Bring the water to a boil over high heat and cook rapidly for 3 to 5 minutes, skimming any foam from the surface. Add the sage and sausage. Reduce the heat and simmer gently for 1 to 2 hours or until the beans are fork-tender (cooked through, but not so soft that they lose their shape). Add additional water to the pan as needed to keep the beans covered.

3. Meanwhile, put the clams, white wine, chopped shallot, and sprigs of thyme in a medium-sized saucepan. Cover and steam over high heat, shaking the pan occasionally, for about 5 minutes or until the clams have opened. Remove from the heat. Discard any clams that remain unopened. Remove the clams from the liquid, cover, and chill thoroughly. Discard the cooking liquid.

4. When the beans are done, drain the contents of the pan into a colander. Remove the sausage and set aside. Discard the sage leaves. Transfer the beans to a small bowl and season to taste with salt and pepper. If not using immediately, allow to cool, cover, and refrigerate.

5. Cut the sausage into small dice. Put in a small bowl. If not using immediately, cover and refrigerate.

6. To serve, bring the clams to room temperature and warm the beans and sausage, if necessary. Place a clam in its bottom shell on a small plate. Top with a few beans and sausage pieces and drizzle with olive oil. Garnish with chopped parsley. Repeat to make 5 to 9 more servings.

YUKON GOLD POTATO CHIPS
WITH WHITE ANCHOVY

serves 6

These potato chips will intrigue your guests. As the chips bake, the anchovy melts into the potato for an intense one-bite amuse. While no one would want to eat a bowl of these chips, a single one packs a flavor punch. I was inspired to make these by David Bouley, the brilliant chef-owner of Bouley Bakery and Danube in New York, who was a guest chef at Tru soon after it opened in 1999. He wove an anchovy between potato slices and fried them. I was hooked and had to develop my own method, which is to thread a white anchovy through slits in a potato slice and then bake the chips in a hot oven until lightly browned. If you can't find white anchovies, use the familiar dark anchovies instead.

1 large Yukon Gold potato or other all-purpose potato 6 white anchovies, patted dry with paper towels	2 tablespoons olive oil Salt and freshly ground black pepper

1. Preheat the oven to 350°F (see Note). Line a baking sheet with a silicone baking mat or parchment paper. Have ready an identical baking sheet and another silicone mat or piece of parchment.

2. Peel the potato. Use a Japanese mandolin or a very sharp knife to cut the potato lengthwise into paper-thin slices.

3. Choose 6 of the largest slices that are most similar in shape. With a sharp paring knife, make 3 small slits in a row in the center of each slice, so that an anchovy can be threaded through along the length.

4. Thread an anchovy fillet through the slits of one slice. Repeat with the remaining anchovies and potato slices. Brush both sides of the chips with olive oil and season to taste with salt and pepper.

5. Arrange the slices on the prepared baking sheet and cover with the second silicone mat or piece of parchment. Top with the second baking sheet and put the sandwiched assembly in the oven. Bake for 10 to 15 minutes or until the chips are golden brown.

6. To serve, season the hot chips with salt and pepper and place each chip on a small plate.

NOTE: If you prefer, deep-fry the chips in canola oil heated to 375°F. Fry the chips until golden brown. Lift from the hot oil with a slotted spoon or spider and drain on paper towels. Season with salt and pepper and serve hot.

meat and poultry
amuse

CRISPY VEAL SWEETBREADS WITH PECANS AND WILD MUSHROOMS

serves 6

The first time I tasted sweetbreads was at Guy Savoy restaurant in Paris more than twenty years ago and I fell in love with them. I later served sweetbreads to my father at Trio, the restaurant where I was executive chef-partner before Tru. He had never eaten them and so was a little skeptical. After one mouthful, he was sold too. I don't think his experience was unique. I have since been on a mission to introduce sweetbreads to others; many people, even serious meat lovers, don't know how to cook or serve sweetbreads. Most people don't even know what they are, and when they hear that they are the thymus glands of calves or lambs, they are not impressed. But this is a shame.

Veal sweetbreads, which are recognized by most as superior to lamb sweetbreads, are just about my favorite food. Cooked correctly, they are crunchy on the outside and moist and creamy on the inside. Find a good butcher and buy those that are encased in a firm, glossy membrane. The thymus glands naturally have one elongated and one rounder lobe—both with the same rich flavor and luxurious texture. Soak the sweetbreads first in milk and then take care not to overcook them. They're earthy, lusty fare—perfect, I think, with wild mushrooms. If you've never cooked them before, a small amuse is a good place to start.

6 veal sweetbreads	¹⁄₄ cup chopped oyster mushrooms
Milk	10 sprigs fresh thyme
2 tablespoons olive oil	Salt and freshly ground black pepper
¹⁄₄ cup chopped shiitake mushrooms	1 cup coarsely chopped toasted
¹⁄₄ cup chopped black trumpet or	pecans
chanterelle mushrooms	Vegetable oil
¹⁄₄ cup chopped lobster, hedgehog,	6 to 8 tablespoons Red Wine Sauce
or cremini mushrooms	(recipe follows)

1. Soak the sweetbreads in milk in the refrigerator for 3 to 4 hours.
2. Lift the sweetbreads from the milk and rinse under cold water. Fill a medium-sized deep skillet about halfway with water and bring the water to a simmer. Add the sweetbreads and blanch for 2 to 3 minutes. Lift from the water with a slotted spoon.

3. | Pat the sweetbreads dry. Trim off any visible fat, membranes, and sinews. Cut them into bite-sized pieces.

4. | Heat the olive oil in a large sauté pan over medium-high heat. When the oil is hot, add the mushrooms and thyme and sauté for 10 to 15 minutes or until the mushrooms are lightly browned and softened.

5. | Remove the pan from the heat and discard the sprigs of thyme. Season to taste with salt and pepper. Toss the mushrooms with the pecans and set aside, covered, to keep warm.

6. | Meanwhile, pour the vegetable oil into a medium-sized deep heavy saucepan to a depth of 2 inches. Heat over high heat until hot and a deep-frying thermometer registers 350°F.

7. | Fry the sweetbreads, in batches, for 5 to 8 minutes or until golden and crisp. Remove from the oil with a slotted spoon or spider. Drain quickly on paper towels; do not allow the sweetbreads to cool very much. Season to taste with salt and pepper.

8. | To serve, divide the sweetbread nuggets among 6 small plates. Spoon red wine sauce around the sweetbreads and top each portion with sautéed wild mushrooms.

RED WINE SAUCE

makes about 1 cup

2 tablespoons unsalted butter	3 cups dry red wine
4 shallots, chopped	4 cups Beef Stock (page 240)
2 to 3 sprigs fresh thyme	Salt and freshly ground black pepper
1 tablespoon black peppercorns	

1. | Melt the butter in a medium-sized, heavy-bottomed saucepan over medium heat. Add the shallots and cook for about 5 minutes or until nicely browned and softened. Add the thyme and the peppercorns and toss well.

2. | Add the red wine and bring to a boil over high heat. Lower the heat and simmer briskly for 30 to 40 minutes or until the red wine is reduced to ½ cup.

3. | Add the beef stock and bring to a boil over high heat. Lower the heat and simmer briskly for 35 to 45 minutes or until the liquid is reduced to 1 cup.

4. | Strain the sauce through a *chinois* or fine-mesh sieve into a small bowl. Season to taste with salt and pepper. Allow to cool. Cover and refrigerate until needed.

5. | Before serving, gently reheat the sauce in a small saucepan over medium heat.

MOROCCAN LAMB WITH
TABBOULEH AND CRISPY GARLIC

serves 6

This was inspired by a meal I ate at Michal Bras, a restaurant owned by the chef of the same name in Laguiole, France. The three-star Michelin restaurant and hotel is built into the side of a cliff, so you have the sensation of hanging over the edge when you dine there.

Lamb, one of the best-tasting meats, is one of the most underappreciated. I love it and have long served it with tabbouleh as a main course. I discovered that the two make a lovely little amuse, *too. Not surprisingly, lamb is at its best in the spring and summer, as are the tomatoes and parsley for the tabbouleh. Bulgur, the classic base for tabbouleh, is cracked and steamed dried wheat berries, and should not be confused with cracked wheat. Bulgur requires little cooking, while cracked wheat must be steamed first to soften it. Finally, the crispy garlic chips with which I garnish this are absolutely delicious and flavor the lamb as only garlic can. If you have time, fry up a lot and serve them as a snack with cocktails.*

½ cup bulgur	1 cup chopped onions
1 tablespoon fresh lemon juice	½ cup chopped carrots
3 tablespoons finely chopped flat-leaf parsley	½ cup chopped celery
	3 tablespoons fresh thyme leaves
2 tablespoons finely diced tomato	2 cups dry red wine
2 tablespoons olive oil	Vegetable oil
Salt and freshly ground black pepper	2 cloves garlic, sliced paper thin
1 pound lamb shank or shoulder	

1. Add the bulgur to a large pot of lightly salted boiling water. Reduce the heat and simmer the bulgur for 10 to 12 minutes or until just tender. Drain the bulgur in a colander. Allow to cool and then transfer to a small shallow bowl.

2. Add the lemon juice, parsley, tomato, and 1 tablespoon of the olive oil and toss until all the grains are coated with the dressing. Season to taste with salt and pepper. Cover and refrigerate.

3. Preheat the oven to 350°F.

4. Heat the remaining 1 tablespoon olive oil in a medium-sized, heavy-bottomed casserole or Dutch oven over medium-high heat. When the oil is almost smoking, add the lamb and sear for 8 to 12 minutes or until nicely browned on all sides.

5. While the lamb is browning, add the onions, carrots, and celery to the pan along with the thyme. Stir the vegetables occasionally.

6. Add the red wine and cook until reduced to a few tablespoons. Add enough water to cover the lamb and bring to a boil, stirring the bottom of the pan with a wooden spoon to dissolve any browned solids into the liquid.

7. Remove from the heat and cover the casserole with a tight-fitting lid. Place in the center of the oven and cook for 1 hour or until the meat is tender and almost falling off the bone. Set aside and allow to cool. When cool, refrigerate the lamb until serving. Discard the vegetables and herbs.

8. Pour the vegetable oil into a small, deep saucepan to a depth of 1½ inches. Heat over medium heat until a deep-frying thermometer registers 325°F.

9. Fry the garlic slices in the oil for 1 to 2 minutes or until they turn golden. Watch carefully because they fry very quickly. Remove from the oil with a slotted spoon to a paper towel to drain. Transfer to a flat plate, season with salt, and allow to cool completely. As they cool, the fried garlic slices will become very crispy.

10. To serve, pull or cut the meat from the bone and cut into small pieces. Place some of the tabbouleh on each of 6 small plates along with some of the lamb. Top each serving with crispy garlic.

makes 25 gougères

Gougères *are savory little puffs flavored with cheese that originated in Sens, France— although similar puffs were made in other regions. Fill them with anything having a creamy consistency, such as goat cheese, ricotta cheese, chicken liver mousse, lobster salad, or, as here, duck liver mousse.*

If you have never made choux paste, which this dough resembles, making the gougères may seem foreign. But they are not difficult. Expect the dough to be stiff, and don't shy away from using a pastry bag. The recipe yields perhaps more little puffs than you need, but it's not feasible to make a smaller batch. Besides, once you and your guests taste these, you'll want to eat more than one. They make wonderful passed hors d'oeuvres, too, and you can alter the size of the gougères according to your need. If you can, fill the gougères from the bottom using a pastry bag. This looks prettier than slicing off the tops and spooning in the filling.

¼ cup foie gras *torchon* (see page 138)	Salt and freshly ground black pepper
4 ounces cream cheese, softened	25 *gougères* (recipe follows)

1. Put the foie gras and cream cheese in a food processor fitted with the metal chopping blade and puree. Transfer to a small bowl and season to taste with salt and pepper.

2. Slice the top third off each *gougère*. Spread a small amount of the mousse on the bottom and then replace the top of the *gougère*. Alternatively, using a plain ¼-inch pastry tip, pierce the bottom of each *gougère*. Insert the tip in a small pastry bag, fill the bag with the mousse, then fill the *gougère*.

3. Place each *gougère* on a small plate and serve.

GOUGÈRE

makes 25 gougères

1 cup milk	4 large eggs
4 tablespoons (½ stick) unsalted butter, cut into chunks	1 cup grated Fol Epi, young Swiss, or Gruyère cheese
1 teaspoon salt	2 teaspoons Dijon mustard
1 cup all-purpose flour, sifted	1 teaspoon dry mustard
½ teaspoon freshly ground pepper	

1. If planning to bake immediately, preheat the oven to 400°F. Line 2 large baking sheets with parchment paper. If baking both sheets at the same time, position 2 oven racks so that one is in the top third of the oven and the other is in the bottom third. Otherwise, position 1 rack in the center of the oven.

2. Combine the milk, butter, and salt in a medium-sized saucepan over medium-low heat. Cook, stirring occasionally, until the butter is melted. Raise the heat and bring to a full boil.

3. Immediately remove the pan from the heat and add the flour all at once, along with the pepper. Stir vigorously with a wooden spoon until the dough is smooth.

4. Return the saucepan to medium heat and cook, stirring constantly with the spoon, for about 2 minutes or until the dough comes away from the sides and gathers in the center of the pan. There will be a thin film of dough on the bottom of the pan.

5. Transfer the dough to the bowl of an electric mixer fitted with the paddle attachment and allow to cool for 10 to 15 minutes or until room temperature.

6. With the mixer on medium speed, beat in the eggs one at a time, beating well after each addition. Beat in the cheese and both mustards until well mixed.

7. Fit a pastry bag with a plain ½-inch tip and fill the bag about halfway with dough. This may have to be done in batches. Pipe mounds that measure about ¾ inch wide onto the prepared baking pans, leaving about 1 inch between each mound. (If you are planning to bake the *gougères* at some future time, put the filled baking sheet[s] in the freezer.)

8. Bake for 10 minutes. Reduce the oven temperature to 350°F and, if using 2 baking sheets, reverse the positions of the sheets. Continue baking for 5 to 6 minutes or until the *gougères* are golden brown and dry. To test for doneness, remove a *gougère* and split it in half. If the inside is not dry, continue to bake a little longer.

9. Transfer the baking sheet(s) to a wire rack. *Gougères* should be cool before filling.

COLD FOIE GRAS TORCHON WITH PEPPERED PINEAPPLE RELISH, CURRANTS, AND BRIOCHE

—

serves 15

I don't deny that this recipe is more complicated than most others in the book, but for foie gras, it's pretty easy. All you need is time and plenty of kosher or coarse salt. The foie gras is not cooked but instead buried in salt and left to cure for nine to ten hours. The result is sublime!

Foie gras is the fattened liver of geese or ducks that have been raised on a rich diet and force-fed grain (usually corn) during the last five or six weeks before butchering. Although goose foie gras is richer than duck foie gras, both work well here. To earn the grade A label, a liver must weigh at least a pound—most weigh a little more—and be as free of bruising as possible. Look for those that are smooth and pale, with few veins. When cooked or cured, the foie gras will be silken, rich, and indescribably sumptuous.

When I was in Monaco, I tasted foie gras prepared by the world-famous chef Alain Ducasse, who served it with pineapple. Here, I serve it with a peppery relish in which the sweetness of the fruit commingles with the pepper and cuts through the foie gras's fat. I love this served on buttery brioche garnished with slightly sour currants. These can be assembled days ahead of time, which is why I often serve them at large parties. They hold up so well, I encourage you to make them as an hors d'oeuvre.

1½ pounds grade A foie gras

2 teaspoons salt

½ teaspoon freshly ground black pepper

½ teaspoon sugar

½ teaspoon pink salt (sodium nitrate)

1½ teaspoons Grand Marnier or other orange-flavored liqueur

Kosher salt

About ½ cup Peppered Pineapple Relish (recipe follows)

Brioche, homemade (page 248) or from a good bakery

Fresh currants, for garnishing

1. Gently pull the two lobes of the foie gras apart to remove all veins, blood clots, and sinews.
2. In a small bowl, mix together the 2 teaspoons salt, the pepper, the sugar, and the ½ tea-

spoon pink salt. Coat the foie gras with the salt mixture. Sprinkle with the Grand Marnier and then tightly cover the bowl with plastic wrap. Refrigerate for 1 hour.

3. Dampen a 3-foot square of cheesecloth and spread it out on a clean work surface. Place the liver at one end and roll up into a cylinder. Twist the overhanging ends in opposite directions to secure the liver tightly (forming a *torchon*). Tie the ends with kitchen string. Put the foie gras *torchon* in a clean shallow pan and refrigerate for 45 minutes.

4. Cover the bottom of a small pan, such as an 8-inch "brownie pan," with a generous layer of kosher salt. Add the *torchon* and cover with more kosher salt, making sure the liver is completely buried in the salt. Refrigerate for 9 to 10 hours.

5. Remove the *torchon* from the salt and unwrap the cheesecloth. Wrap the foie gras in plastic wrap, set on a plate, and refrigerate for up to 2 days.

6. To serve, use a hot knife to cut the foie gras into ¼-inch-thick slices. Place each slice on a small plate along with some of the pineapple relish, a slice of brioche, and a few currants for garnish.

PEPPERED PINEAPPLE RELISH

makes about 1 cup

1 fresh pineapple	¼ cup firmly packed brown sugar
¼ cup coarsely ground black pepper	

1. Peel, core, and remove the brown "eyes" from the pineapple. Cut the flesh into very fine dice. Put the diced pineapple in a fine-mesh sieve set over a small bowl and allow the juice to drain from the pineapple. You should have about 2 cups of juice. Reserve the juice and flesh separately.

2. Spread the pepper in a dry frying pan and toast over medium-high heat, shaking the pan frequently, for 40 to 50 seconds or until fragrant. Transfer to a plate and allow to cool completely.

3. Put the pineapple juice in a small saucepan and cook over medium heat until reduced by half. Add the brown sugar and stir until dissolved. Allow to cool.

4. Pour the pineapple juice over the reserved diced pineapple and toss. Add the pepper and mix well.

CHILLED AND GRILLED BLACK MISSION FIGS WITH MASCARPONE FOAM AND PROSCIUTTO DI PARMA

serves 6

The name Tramonto means "sunset" in Italian, which makes it fun for me to travel there; I can always find postcards with my name on them. One of the best times I had in Italy was in 2001, when I represented the United States at the International Prosciutto di Parma Festival in Parma, along with representatives from seven other countries. The event celebrated Italy's magnificent ham, or prosciutto. Being in Parma was amazing: It's the home of three of life's greatest luxuries: Parma ham, Parmigiano-Reggiano cheese, and the Ferrari. Rightly so, Italians are purists when it comes to their prosciutto, and so I decided to keep it simple. I paired the ham with figs, which is a classic combination in Parma, and then added mascarpone cheese, an equally classic accompaniment. To sweeten the figs, I grilled them; to lighten the velvety and sinfully rich cheese, I made it into a foam. I am proud to say that the dish placed second in the competition, and I have since modified it as an amuse, which is nothing short of a mouthful of intense flavor and textures.

A taste of authentic Parma ham is all you need to understand why it's revered the world over. Made from the pork of relatively young pigs that are raised on a careful diet in this mountainous region of Italy and then cured with painstaking care for ten to twelve months, the ham is fragrant, not overly salty, and luxuriously streaked with fat. All good ham should be sliced shortly before it's served, and this is particularly true for Parma and other quality prosciutto. It's usually shipped from Italy already cut from the bone but fastidiously wrapped. Slice it paper thin for the best flavor and texture. If you cannot find prosciutto di Parma ham, skip this dish until you can. It's not hard to locate and you'll be glad you waited.

3 fresh Black Mission figs
8 tablespoons (1 stick) unsalted
   butter, melted
¼ cup sugar

Salt and freshly ground black pepper
6 thin slices prosciutto di Parma
1 to 2 tablespoons Mascarpone Foam
   (recipe follows)

1. Slice the figs in half through the stem.
2. Lightly grease a grill pan and heat over medium-high heat.
3. While the pan is heating, put the melted butter in a shallow bowl and the sugar in another. Coat each fig half with melted butter and then roll in the sugar.
4. Grill the coated figs in the hot pan, turning once, for 2 to 3 minutes or until just softened. Season to taste with salt and pepper. Refrigerate until needed.
5. To serve, put a slice of ham on each of 6 small plates. Arrange a fig half on the ham. Shake the foamer vigorously and garnish each fig with a small dab of mascarpone foam. Wrap the ends of the ham slice around the fig and mascarpone foam.

MASCARPONE FOAM

makes about 4 cups

1 cup mascarpone cheese	Salt and freshly ground black pepper
3 cups chilled heavy cream	

1. Put the mascarpone cheese in a medium-sized bowl and soften it by gently folding it over on itself with a rubber spatula. Slowly mix in the cream so that the mixture is smooth and the cream is thoroughly incorporated. Season to taste with salt and pepper.
2. Pour the mixture into the chilled canister of a foamer. Charge with 1 or 2 charges. Chill before using.

serves 6

Just one bite of this amuse *transports you to the south of France, where sun-drenched fields yield ripe, juicy tomatoes, great capers, and tangy olives, and where the lamb is sweet and tender. This* amuse *is made elegant with a truffle vinaigrette, although it's equally delicious with a black olive vinaigrette. Drying late-summer's best tomatoes is a good alternative to canning or freezing them. The process leaves them exceptionally sweet. You can serve them on their own, pack them in oil, or use them in this lovely dish.*

3 Roma tomatoes (about 1 pound) or other good, firm, ripe tomatoes

1 clove garlic, chopped

1 tablespoon olive oil

1 teaspoon chopped flat-leaf parsley

1 teaspoon chopped fresh basil

1 tablespoon sweet Hungarian paprika

1 teaspoon freshly ground black pepper

6 ounces loin of lamb, cut with the grain

Salt

3 tablespoons Truffle Vinaigrette (page 244)

1. Preheat the oven to 250°F.

2. Core and split the tomatoes in half lengthwise. Transfer to a medium-sized bowl and gently toss with the garlic, oil, parsley, and basil.

3. Lift the tomatoes from the bowl and place, cut side up, on a baking sheet. Roast for 3 hours. They will be somewhat dried but still slightly plump. Cool to room temperature.

4. Combine the paprika and pepper in a small bowl and mix well. Coat the lamb with the spice mixture and then season to taste with salt.

5. Heat a lightly greased cast-iron skillet over high heat until almost smoking. Cook the lamb for about 1 minute on each side or until well browned. Transfer the lamb to a plate and allow to rest for 5 minutes.

6. To serve, slice the lamb into 6 equal portions. Cut each oven-dried tomato half lengthwise in half again. Arrange 2 pieces of tomato on a small plate. Spoon some of the truffle vinaigrette alongside the tomatoes and place a slice of lamb over the vinaigrette. Repeat to make 5 more servings.

WARM MINI FOIE GRAS
CLUB SANDWICH

serves 4

I am truly passionate about searching the world for the greatest club sandwich ever made. I am a major fan of sandwiches, and club sandwiches are my all-time favorites. I grew up eating them, and later when I worked at the Strathallen Hotel in Rochester, New York, I made a lot of them for room service. When I travel, I order them from diners, coffee shops, delis, and sandwich shops and inevitably from hotel room service. Over the years, I have kept an informal rating of those I like best. At the top of the chart is the club sandwich served on the Queen Elizabeth II. *I think I ordered one every night from cabin service when I was a guest chef on the ship on a sailing from London to New York.*

When I wanted to create a small, sophisticated club sandwich to serve as an amuse, I turned to foie gras and rich, buttery homemade brioche. These miniature sand-wiches use only small slices of sautéed foie gras, which means you can get a taste without spending a fortune. I like to make this with goose liver foie gras, but duck liver foie gras is also flavorful.

½ pound foie gras

12 slices brioche, homemade
   (page 248) or from a good bakery

½ cup Pesto Aioli (recipe follows)

1 tomato, very thinly sliced

About 4 ounces microsprouts, tender
   mesclun greens, or small leaves
   of Bibb lettuce

1. With a sharp knife, cut the foie gras into 8 slices.
2. Heat a dry cast-iron skillet over medium-high heat. When hot, sauté the foie gras for about 1 minute on each side or until lightly browned. Drain on paper towels.
3. Use 3 slices of brioche for each sandwich.
4. Assemble each sandwich by spreading aioli on each slice of brioche. Top the bottom slice of brioche with a slice of foie gras, a tomato slice, some microsprouts, and another slice of bread. Top this with another slice of foie gras, another tomato slice, and more sprouts. Lay the third slice of brioche on top, aioli side down. Repeat for each sandwich. Cut in half and serve.

PESTO AIOLI

5 large egg yolks

½ cup olive oil

1 tablespoon fresh lemon juice

About 4 ounces fresh basil leaves

1 clove garlic

2 tablespoons pine nuts

2 tablespoons grated Parmigiano-
  Reggiano cheese

2 tablespoons olive, canola, or
  grapeseed oil

Salt and freshly ground black pepper

1. Put the egg yolks in a small bowl and whisk with a wire whisk. Whisking constantly, slowly add ¼ cup oil. Begin very slowly, a few drops at a time. When the oil is emulsified, add the remaining ¼ cup oil in a steady stream.

2. Stir the lemon juice into the mayonnaise. Set aside.

3. Put the basil leaves, garlic, pine nuts, and cheese in a food processor fitted with a metal blade. With the machine running, add the 2 tablespoons oil and process until emulsified.

4. Stir the basil mixture into the mayonnaise. Season to taste with salt and pepper. Use immediately or cover and refrigerate for up to 3 days. Whisk before using.

WARM TRUFFLED
OXTAIL TARTLETS

serves 6

Since I opened Tru, I have served sturgeon with braised oxtail in a red wine sauce, which has been and always will be one of our signature dishes. Other than braised lamb shanks, braised oxtail is my favorite braised meat—it's a shame it's so underutilized. I encourage you to try it! The robustly flavored oxtail accents the meaty fish to a T, which some might find surprising. Oxtail, not unlike lamb shanks and short ribs, falls from the bone in mouthwatering shreds after it's braised in an aromatic broth for several hours. Here, I pair it with a spiced sweet carrot puree to emphasize the earthy flavors of autumn, and serve the amuse in tiny tartlet shells. This may seem like a lot of work for such small bites, but when you read the recipe, you will see it requires more time than effort. I also think this is an outstanding way to learn about cooking the humble oxtail. You can toss the meat with pasta, make a risotto, or even serve it with fish—as I do with sturgeon.

6 pounds oxtails	2 cups dry Madeira wine
2 tablespoons black peppercorns	2 cups dry red wine
3 tablespoons vegetable oil	8 cups Beef Stock (page 240)
1 cup red pearl onions	½ cup water
5 carrots, the 2 largest cut into large dice and the remaining 3 coarsely chopped	Salt and freshly ground black pepper
	1 whole clove
	Pinch of ground cinnamon
2 ribs celery, cut into large dice	6 tartlet shells (see page 249)

1. Trim the oxtails of any visible fat. Using a sharp paring knife, score the tails lengthwise. Set aside.

2. Cut an 8-inch square of cheesecloth and mound the peppercorns in the center of the square. Bring the corners of the cloth together and tie the sachet with kitchen string.

3. Heat the oil in a large, heavy-bottomed casserole or Dutch oven over medium-high heat. When the oil is almost smoking, add the oxtails and cook for 12 to 15 minutes or until they are well browned on all sides, working in batches if necessary. Remove the oxtails from the pan and set aside.

4. Reduce the heat to medium and add the onions, the diced carrots, and the celery to the pan. Cook, stirring for 8 to 10 minutes, or until the vegetables are golden brown.

5. Preheat the oven to 300°F.

6. Add the Madeira, red wine, and peppercorn sachet to the pan and bring to a boil over medium-high heat while stirring the bottom of the pan with a wooden spoon to scrape up any browned solids and dissolve them into the liquid. Reduce the heat slightly and simmer for about 15 minutes or until the liquid is reduced by half.

7. Return the oxtails to the pan, add the beef stock, and bring to a boil over medium-high heat. Remove from the heat and cover the casserole with a tight-fitting lid. Place in the center of the oven and cook for 3 to 4 hours or until the meat is tender and almost falling off the bone.

8. Remove and discard the peppercorn sachet from the casserole. Remove the oxtails and set aside to cool at room temperature. Then, transfer them to a large bowl, cover, and refrigerate until chilled.

9. Meanwhile, skim the fat from the surface of the braising liquid. Put the pan over medium-high heat and bring the liquid to a boil. Reduce the heat slightly and simmer for about 35 minutes or until the liquid is reduced by half.

10. While the liquid is reducing, put the chopped carrots in a small saucepan and cover with cold water. Bring to a boil over high heat and boil for 10 minutes or until fork-tender. Drain the carrots and transfer to a heavy-duty blender or food processor.

11. Add about ¼ cup of the water to the blender or processor and puree. With the motor running, slowly add as much of the remaining ¼ cup water as needed for a fluid consistency.

12. Scrape the puree into a small bowl and season to taste with salt and pepper. Mix in the clove and cinnamon.

13. Strain the puree through a *chinois* or fine-mesh sieve into another small bowl. (If not using right away, allow to cool, cover, and refrigerate until needed. Before serving, gently reheat the sauce in a small saucepan over medium heat.)

14. Pick the meat off the bones of the chilled oxtails and discard the bones. Return the meat to the casserole and season to taste with salt and pepper. If not serving immediately, allow the braising liquid to cool to room temperature. Cover and refrigerate.

15. To serve, reheat as much of the oxtail braise as needed in a small saucepan. Spread a thin layer of the carrot puree over the bottom of each tartlet shell. Fill the shells with the warm oxtail mixture and transfer each filled tartlet to a small plate.

ROASTED PORK TENDERLOIN
WITH ROSEMARY AND APPLES

serves 6

Everyone has seen pictures of a roasted suckling pig with an apple in its mouth. Like so many garnishes, that apple has a direct relationship to the dish. The meat from hogs fed on a diet rich in apples is reckoned to be about the sweetest pork on earth. Most of us have little idea of the dietary history of the pork we buy, but the sweet, tender meat has an affinity for apples and other fruit, which is why I spread the meat with a mildly spicy apple filling and serve it with a simple apple-and-herb salad.

Pork tenderloin, cut from the center loin, cooks quickly and tastes light and fresh. Buy pork with pinkish meat and firm white fat. Cook it just until a meat thermometer registers 150°F and then let it rest to avoid overcooking. I serve this amuse *during the holidays, as its flavors blend perfectly with others of traditional celebratory meals. I have even served this on Thanksgiving and for many other holidays. I love pork—it truly is "the other white meat" in my kitchen. Thank you, Pork Council.*

4 Granny Smith or other large tart apples	1 cup brioche crumbs, from homemade brioche (page 248) or brioche from a good bakery
2 sprigs fresh rosemary	4 tablespoons olive oil
1 tablespoon unsalted butter	1 tablespoon sherry wine vinegar
1 cinnamon stick	Salt and freshly ground black pepper
	6 to 8 ounces pork tenderloin

1. Peel, core, and cut 3 of the apples into very fine dice.

2. Strip the leaves from 1 of the rosemary sprigs and finely chop the leaves.

3. Melt the butter in a small sauté pan over medium heat. Add the diced apples, the chopped rosemary, and the cinnamon stick and cook for 1 minute. Set aside to cool. Discard the cinnamon stick. When cool, toss with the crumbs. Set the apple filling aside while you make the salad and prepare the pork.

4. Peel and core the remaining apple and then cut it into very fine dice. Put the dice in a small bowl.

5. Strip the leaves from the remaining rosemary sprig and finely chop them.

6. Add 3 tablespoons of the oil and the vinegar to the diced apple and toss. Season to taste with salt and pepper. Scatter the chopped rosemary over the apple and mix well. Set the salad aside.

7. Preheat the oven to 350°F.

8. Cut the pork lengthwise without cutting all the way through. Open up the pork and pound the meat to form a rectangle of even thickness. Spread a thin layer of the cooled apple filling down the center and fold over the sides to form a compact cylinder. Tie with kitchen string.

9. Heat the remaining 1 tablespoon oil in a small ovenproof sauté pan over medium-high heat until almost smoking. Sear the pork on all sides until well browned.

10. Transfer the pan to the oven and roast the pork for 8 to 10 minutes or until medium and an instant-read thermometer registers 150°F. Transfer the pork to a plate and allow to rest for 5 minutes.

11. To serve, slice the pork into 6 equal portions. Spoon some apple-rosemary salad on a small plate and place a slice of pork alongside. Repeat to make 5 more servings.

SEARED CUMIN-CRUSTED SQUAB
WITH HUCKLEBERRY GASTRIQUE

serves 6

Squab—tiny, gamy-tasting birds—are easiest to find in the late fall and winter, although you may have to order them from a specialty butcher. The rich, tender meat packs enough flavor to stand up nicely to cumin, which I also like with lamb. Huckleberries may be harder to find, although they are similar to blueberries. Their tartness works well with the potency of cumin and the lusciousness of the squab. The beautiful complexity of the huckleberries makes them a match made in heaven with this hearty squab. Gastriques are full-flavored accompaniments to meat and poultry, not unlike a relish or chutney, and this one was first put together with the help of Jason Robinson, one of my sous-chefs.

¼ cup French green lentils, rinsed and drained	½ teaspoon ground cumin, plus more for sprinkling
1 tablespoon finely diced onion	Salt and freshly ground black pepper
1 tablespoon finely diced carrot	1 to 2 tablespoons Huckleberry
1 tablespoon finely diced celery	Gastrique (recipe follows)
4 cups lightly salted water	6 sprigs fresh thyme, for garnishing
1 boneless squab breast, skin on	

1. In a small saucepan, combine the lentils, onion, carrot, and celery and pour the water over them. Bring to a boil, reduce the heat, and simmer for 25 to 30 minutes or until the vegetables are tender but not soft. Drain the lentils into a colander and transfer to a small bowl. Cover and set aside to keep warm.

2. Coat the squab all over with the cumin and season to taste with salt and pepper.

3. Heat a small sauté pan over medium-high heat. When the pan is hot, sear the squab breast, skin side down, for 3 to 4 minutes or until the skin is golden brown and crisp. Turn and cook for 1 to 2 minutes longer until the meat is medium. Transfer to a plate and allow to rest for 5 minutes.

4. To serve, slice the squab into 6 equal portions. Spoon some of the lentils onto a small plate and top with a slice of squab. Surround the lentils with a drizzle of huckleberry *gastrique*. Garnish each dish with a thyme sprig and dust the plate with a little cumin. Repeat to make 5 more servings.

HUCKLEBERRY GASTRIQUE

makes about ¹/₂ cup

1 cup dry red wine	¹/₄ cup apple cider vinegar
¹/₂ cup sugar	1 cup huckleberries or blueberries
1 tablespoon water	

1. Bring the wine to a boil in a small nonreactive saucepan over medium-high heat. Cook for about 20 minutes or until the wine is reduced to ¹/₄ cup.

2. Combine the sugar and water in a small, heavy-bottomed saucepan. Stir until the sugar is evenly moistened. Cook over medium-low heat, without stirring, for 3 to 5 minutes or until the sugar is completely melted and caramelized. When the sugar begins to caramelize, swirl the pan to even out the color.

3. Off the heat, carefully pour the vinegar into the sugar all at once. The mixture will bubble up. Return to the heat and whisk constantly until the caramel is smooth and well blended. Add the reduced red wine and the huckleberries. Simmer over low heat for about 15 minutes or until reduced to ¹/₂ cup. Serve at once or cover and refrigerate for up to 2 days. Warm gently before using.

BRESAOLA CROSTINI WITH WHITE TRUFFLE OIL AND PECORINO

serves 6

My maternal grandfather, Enzo Gentile, who emigrated from Naples, Italy, may have been a barber by trade, but his true love was enjoying the varied and tempting cuisine of his homeland. He thought nothing of making his own red wine and curing his own meat such as sopressata, coppa, salami, and bresaola in the basement beneath his barbershop in up-state New York. As a boy, I was well aware of the time and care that went into products such as bresaola. This is cured and air-dried beef that, while not terribly salty, is imbued with an intoxicating aroma and mellow flavor. Although first produced in the north of Italy, nowadays you can find it throughout the country, and as delicious as it may be, no bre-saola I have tasted compares with my grandfather's. Like so many other Italian cured meats, this is best sliced paper thin and served simply. It's exquisite with a squeeze of lemon juice, a drizzle of extra-virgin olive oil, and a grind of pepper, but I like to dress it up a little with white truffle oil and the best pecorino cheese I can find.

Six ¼-inch-thick slices bread, cut from a baguette	4 ounces pecorino cheese
4 ounces bresaola, sliced paper thin	2 tablespoons white truffle oil
	Snipped fresh chives, for garnishing

1. Toast both sides of the bread under the broiler or in a toaster until golden brown.
2. Divide the bresaola evenly among the toasted baguette slices. Using a vegetable peeler, shave the pecorino cheese over the meat. Garnish the *crostini* with a drizzle of the truffle oil and a sprinkling of chives and serve.

VENISON CARPACCIO WITH CHOCOLATE SAUCE AND CHAMPAGNE GRAPES

serves 6

I have enormous respect for fellow Chicago restaurateur Rick Bayless, whose knowledge of Mexican cuisine is surpassed only by his ability to cook it. I freely admit that this dish was inspired after eating chicken with mole at Rick's restaurants, Frontera Grill and Topolobampo. I took the idea back to my kitchen, where I decided to try a similar sauce with venison.

Loin of venison is the preferred cut from this most popular of game meats—and, believe it or not, it is the most popular entrée on the menu at Tru. Often, the loin is cut into chops or steaks and then grilled or broiled. I prefer to char venison loin to accentuate its smokiness and earthiness, two characteristics that blend nicely with the barely sweet chocolate sauce. Once it's charred, I chill it and serve it thinly sliced to mimic classic carpaccio.

6 to 8 ounces loin of venison	Fleur de Sel or other high-quality sea
1 teaspoon ground cumin	salt
1 tablespoon whole espresso beans	Champagne grapes or other sweet,
½ cup semisweet chocolate chips	ripe red grapes, for garnishing
1 tablespoon water	Dill oil or other herb-infused oil

1. Trim the venison of all sinews and visible fat.

2. Put the cumin and coffee beans in a spice grinder and grind to a powder. Rub the spice mixture over the venison.

3. Heat a dry cast-iron skillet or sauté pan over high heat until very hot. Sear the venison on each side for about 30 seconds, being sure to keep the center raw. Transfer to a plate and refrigerate immediately to cool the meat quickly.

4. Spread a large sheet of plastic wrap on a work surface. Place the chilled venison loin at one end of the plastic wrap and roll up into a cylinder. Twist the overhanging ends of the plastic wrap in opposite directions to secure the venison tightly. Tie the ends with kitchen string. Put the venison in the freezer for several hours until completely frozen.

5. Put the chocolate in the top of a double boiler or in a heatproof bowl that will fit over a small saucepan. Set aside. Fill the bottom of the double boiler or the saucepan halfway with water and bring to a boil; turn off the heat. Place the chocolate over the hot water and let stand for a few seconds or until the chocolate starts to melt. Stir until completely melted. Add the water to thin out the sauce if desired. Keep warm.

6. Unwrap the venison and cut 12 paper-thin slices from the meat. If you have an electric meat slicer, use it. Otherwise, use a sharp knife. If the meat is too hard to slice, let it thaw for a few minutes. As soon as it's sliced, it will begin to thaw, so it will be at the perfect temperature when served.

7. To serve, use a pastry brush to paint a small amount of chocolate sauce on each of 6 small plates. Arrange 2 slices of venison over the sauce and garnish each serving with Champagne grapes. Drizzle the venison with dill oil.

RICK'S "LINGUINE AND CLAMS"

serves 6 to 10

My mom's family was from Abruzzi, Italy, and my dad's from Naples, which means I was destined to make great linguine with clams—until I met my wife, Eileen Carroll, who makes even better linguine and clams than I do. When I began developing amuse-bouche *at Tru, I put a contemporary spin on this by cutting a cucumber to look like linguine to create an illusion that works with the clams for a light spring dish.*

Always buy clams from a reputable merchant. If you buy them from a roadside truck or stand, you can't be sure they were harvested in clean waters. Make sure hard-shell clams, such as littleneck, cherrystone, and Manila, are tightly closed; if one is gaping open, poke it. If it doesn't snap closed, don't cook it. Cherrystones are a little larger than littlenecks. For this recipe, be sure you are buying Atlantic littlenecks; Pacific littlenecks are a bit tougher. Manila clams, also called Japanese clams, tiny and sweet, taste great here.

½ to ¾ pound littleneck, cherrystone, or Manila clams, rinsed and scrubbed	1 bunch fresh thyme
	1 cucumber, peeled
	1 cup diced Cucumber Aspic
1 cup dry white wine	(page 250)
1 shallot, finely chopped	

1. Put the clams in a medium-sized saucepan with the white wine, chopped shallot, and sprigs of thyme. Cover the pan and steam over high heat, shaking the pan occasionally, for about 5 minutes or until all the clams have opened. Using a slotted spoon, lift the clams from the cooking broth and discard any that have not opened. Refrigerate until thoroughly chilled.

2. Using a Japanese mandolin fitted with the fine-shredding blade, julienne the cucumber lengthwise, avoiding the seedy center part. If you don't have a mandolin, slice the cucumber lengthwise into very thin slices using a sharp knife.

3. In a saucepan filled with lightly salted simmering water, blanch the cucumber for 30 seconds. Drain and immediately submerge in cold water. Drain again and transfer to a small bowl to cool.

4. To serve, leave the clams in their bottom shells. Twirl a small, pretty seafood fork in the cucumber, securing enough for 1 portion. Lay the fork on top of a clam on a small plate. Garnish with diced cucumber aspic. Repeat to make 5 to 9 more servings.

serves 6

If you start with high-quality hamachi or yellowfin tuna, it is hard to miss with this dish. The quality of the fish is what this is all about. You will end up with very clean, buttery tartare—one that is satisfyingly rich and fun to serve. If you can't find hamachi, which is young yellowtail tuna, substitute another tuna, or salmon, snapper, or swordfish. A spoonful of this one-bite amuse is all you need, particularly when it's garnished with silken crème fraîche. I like to serve tartare on a mirror, whether it's a mirrored tray or a utility shelf or a tile from the hardware store. It's almost like a funhouse effect: The reflected food keeps on going and going!

½ pound sushi-quality hamachi or yellowfin tuna

½ red onion

1 tablespoon finely chopped kaffir lime leaves

1½ teaspoons fresh lime juice

1½ teaspoons fresh lemon juice

Salt and freshly ground black pepper

¼ cup crème fraîche, homemade (page 252) or store-bought

½ teaspoon hijiki seaweed

1. Cut the hamachi into very small dice. Mince the red onion very fine to measure about ½ cup. Toss the hamachi and onion together in a small glass or ceramic bowl along with the lime leaves.

2. Add the citrus juices and toss gently. Season to taste with salt and pepper and refrigerate for no longer than 15 minutes.

3. Mound some tartare mixture in the bowl of a large dessert spoon or another decorative spoon. Using a second spoon of the same size, form the tartare into an oval, or quenelle. Remove the top spoon. The tartare will be served on the first spoon.

4. To serve, spread a thin layer of crème fraîche over the tartare and garnish with some of the hijiki. Repeat to make 5 more spoons. Arrange the spoons on a mirror.

SPOON OF LOBSTER SEVICHE
WITH LOBSTER OIL AND
LOBSTER ROE

serves 6

Norman Van Aken, chef-owner of Norman's Restaurant, has always been a great friend and inspiration in the kitchen, but as much as I admire the cooking of Miami's acclaimed chef, I am not what you'd call a nuevo Latino *guy. Nevertheless, this seviche is a tribute to many that Norman makes, while still being typical of the food I serve at Tru.*

You can make this amuse *with any fish, but I use lobster because it's so elegant and flavorful. The acid in the marinade sets the palate salivating with anticipation—all you need is a little bite. The delicate lobster can be served on a spoon or a fork, or in lobster-tail shells. Toss the lobster meat with clams and serve on clam shells.*

1 red bell pepper	Juice of ½ orange
1 yellow bell pepper	1 tablespoon finely chopped fresh
½ red onion	cilantro
1 pound cooked lobster meat, from	Salt and freshly ground black pepper
the tails of three 1-pound lobsters	Lobster Oil (recipe follows)
(see Notes on pages 95 and 167)	Lobster Roe (recipe follows),
½ cup mirin	for garnishing
½ cup olive oil	Six 2-inch-long chive pieces,
¼ cup fresh lemon juice	for garnishing
¼ cup fresh lime juice	

1. Remove the ribs and seeds from the peppers. Mince very fine. Mince the red onion very fine. Chop the lobster meat very fine. Toss the peppers, onion, and lobster together in a glass or ceramic bowl.

2. Add the mirin, oil, and citrus juices to the lobster mixture. Toss gently. Add the cilantro and toss gently. Season with salt and pepper and refrigerate for no more than 30 minutes.

3. To serve, scoop the lobster seviche onto 6 decorative spoons. Arrange each spoon on a small plate. Drizzle with lobster oil and garnish each plate with lobster roe and a piece of chive.

LOBSTER OIL

makes about 2½ cups

2½ cups grapeseed oil   ¼ cup annatto seeds
2 to 3 pounds lobster shells
(see Note)

1. Heat about 2 tablespoons of the oil in a large pot over medium-high heat. Add the lobster shells and sauté for 2 to 3 minutes or until red.
2. Transfer to a food processor in batches and process into small pieces.
3. Return the ground shells to the pot. Add the seeds and the remaining oil and bring to a simmer. As soon as the oil is hot, remove the pot from the heat and set aside to cool to room temperature.
4. Strain the cooled oil through a coffee filter or *chinois* into a glass container. Cover and refrigerate until ready to use. The oil lasts for 2 to 3 months in the refrigerator.

NOTE: Ask the fishmonger for leftover uncooked lobster shells or save those from the lobsters you use to make the seviche. Any leftover lobster shells must be rinsed to rid them of meat, cartilage, and other material. Clean and dry shells can be frozen for 4 to 6 months. They add great flavor to bisques and pasta sauces.

LOBSTER ROE

makes about ½ cup

Roe from 1 lobster (see Note)

1. Preheat the oven to 150°F.

2. Spread the roe in a shallow baking pan and allow to dry and turn red in the oven, about 1 hour.

3. Transfer the roe to a fine-mesh sieve or *tamis* and rub gently so that the roe turns into a coarse powder.

4. Refrigerate in a tightly lidded container for 2 to 3 months.

NOTE: Lobster roe is sold in small jars in specialty stores and you can use it here. You may find it at fish markets, too. You won't need much, so buy a small 4- to 6-ounce container.

CHICKPEA SPOON WITH FETA AND ROASTED GARLIC

serves 6

When I make this, I think of my mom, Gloria, who made delicious cold chickpea salads every summer to take to the picnics and cookouts she so enjoyed. I fondly recall her chickpea and feta cheese salad, and developed this in her memory. I urge you to find a creamy feta cheese with just the right salt content. Most feta is made from sheep's milk, but it can also be made with goat and cow milk. Some ardently believe the best comes from Greece, but others prefer Bulgarian, Turkish, French, or Italian feta. There's very good feta made in the United States. It's not a complex cheese, but when correctly made, it crumbles pleasantly even as it slices. As a departure, you could whip the chickpeas in a food processor, pile the puree on a spoon, and serve it with feta crumbled over it.

1 cup dried chickpeas	Salt and freshly ground black pepper
1 rib celery, chopped	1 red bell pepper
1 carrot, chopped	1/2 cup couscous
1/2 small onion, chopped	1/2 cup chopped flat-leaf parsley
2 heads garlic, unpeeled	1/2 cup chopped fresh oregano
1/4 cup olive oil, plus more as needed	3/4 cup crumbled feta cheese

1. Put the chickpeas in a large bowl and add enough cold water to cover by several inches. Soak the chickpeas for at least 6 hours or overnight. Drain and transfer to a large saucepan or a stockpot.

2. Cut a 10-inch square of cheesecloth and mound the celery, carrot, and onion in the center of the square. Bring the corners of the cloth together and tie the sachet with kitchen string.

3. Add enough cold water to cover the chickpeas by 3 inches. Add the vegetable sachet. Bring to a boil over high heat and boil rapidly for 3 to 5 minutes, skimming any foam that rises to the surface. Reduce the heat and simmer gently for 45 minutes to 1 hour or until the chickpeas are tender and cooked through. Add additional water to the pan as needed to keep the chickpeas covered.

4. Drain the contents of the pan into a colander. Remove and discard the vegetable sachet.

Transfer the chickpeas to a large bowl and allow them to cool to room temperature. Cover and refrigerate.

5.   Preheat the oven to 300°F.

6.   Slice the pointed tops off the garlic heads and brush the exposed pulp with oil so that it is well coated. Wrap the heads securely in aluminum foil and arrange in a small baking pan. Roast for about 1 hour or until the garlic is soft. Allow to cool and then refrigerate if not using immediately.

7.   Gently squeeze the bottoms of the garlic heads so that the softened pulp is extracted from the individual cloves. Discard the skins. Put the pulp in a small bowl and mash with a wooden spoon until pureed. While mashing, add enough oil to achieve a saucelike consistency. Season to taste with salt and pepper. Cover and refrigerate until ready to use.

8.   Preheat the broiler.

9.   Put the bell pepper on a broiling tray and broil for 10 to 15 minutes, turning several times, until the pepper is softened and the skin is charred and blistered. Alternatively, hold the pepper over a gas flame, turning it to char the skin. Put the charred pepper in a small bowl, cover with plastic wrap, and allow to steam for about 10 minutes. Using your fingers, rub the charred skin from the cooled pepper. Cut the flesh into strips and remove and discard the seeds and ribs. Cut the flesh into ½-inch dice.

10. In a large pot of boiling water, cook the couscous for 3 to 5 minutes or until tender. Drain the couscous in a *chinois* or fine-mesh sieve and transfer to a medium-sized bowl. Use a fork to fluff up the grains. Cover and refrigerate until chilled.

11. Add the couscous to the bowl of chickpeas and toss with the roasted pepper, the parsley, the oregano, and the ¼ cup oil. Season to taste with salt and pepper.

12. To serve, spread a dab of garlic sauce in the bowl of a decorative tablespoon. Top with a mound of chickpea salad—about ¼ cup per serving—and garnish with a sprinkling of feta cheese. Repeat to make 5 more servings.

ASIAN SOBA NOODLE FORK
WITH WATER CHESTNUTS

serves 6

No amuse is more appealing and fun than this one of Asian noodles twirled around a fork. When I was growing up, my mother cooked pasta on Sundays for as long as I can remember, as did most Italian home cooks. When my father and I dipped into the food cooking on the stove, my mom constantly chided us to "take just a forkful!" When I was creating this amuse, I thought of my mother's words and tried serving one on a fork. After a little experimentation, I discovered that soba *noodles worked beautifully—not as heavy as linguine and with a delightful texture. When tossed with this sauce, the noodles explode with flavor.*

I like this sauce so much, I keep a jar of it at all times in my home refrigerator to toss on noodles, use as a marinade for chicken, beef, or pork, and even sprinkle over greens as a salad dressing. I got the idea for it from a noodle shop on Copperwell Street in San Francisco, where noodles were served at a small counter. The owner sold bottles of a sauce quite like this; I bought a few, took them back to my kitchen, and worked out something similar.

One 16-ounce package *soba* noodles	1 yellow bell pepper, seeded and
One 8-ounce can water chestnuts,	julienned
drained and very thinly sliced	1 carrot, julienned
10 fresh snow peas, julienned	About 1 cup Copperwell Noodle
1 red bell pepper, seeded and	Sauce (recipe follows)
julienned	6 shavings of pecorino cheese

1. In a saucepan filled with lightly salted boiling water, cook the noodles for 2 to 3 minutes or until al dente. Drain and rinse under cold running water. Drain again.

2. Transfer the cool noodles to a medium bowl. Add the water chestnuts, snow peas, red and yellow peppers, and carrot and toss to mix. Sprinkle the sauce over the noodles and toss until the noodles are coated but not wet. Do not use more sauce than needed.

3. To serve, twirl a decorative fork in the noodles, securing enough for 1 generous bite. Lay the fork on a small plate and garnish with a shaving of pecorino cheese. Repeat to make 5 more servings.

NOTE: Use a potato peeler to make single shavings of cheese. Pull the peeler over the top of a hunk of cheese to make each shaving.

COPPERWELL NOODLE SAUCE

makes about 3 cups

1¼ cups organic soy sauce

¼ cup red wine vinegar

2 teaspoons sesame oil

1½ cups minced scallions, white and
   green parts

2 teaspoons crushed Szechuan
   peppercorns

2½ cups vegetable oil

1½ teaspoons ground cayenne
   pepper

¼ cup packed light brown sugar

¼ cup crushed sesame seeds

1. In a small nonreactive bowl, combine the soy sauce, vinegar, sesame oil, scallions, and peppercorns and stir gently.

2. In a large saucepan, heat 1⅔ cups of the vegetable oil over high heat until very hot. When the oil bubbles, carefully sprinkle the cayenne over it. Immediately remove the pan from the heat and allow the oil to cool slightly. Pour the oil into the bowl and stir well.

3. Heat the remaining vegetable oil in the same saucepan over high heat. When hot, remove from the heat and stir the brown sugar into the oil until dissolved. Take care, as the oil might spatter when the sugar is added. Add to the bowl and stir well.

4. Spread the sesame seeds in a dry frying pan and toast over medium-high heat for 40 to 50 seconds or until they darken a shade and are fragrant. Transfer to a plate to stop cooking and allow to cool completely.

5. Stir the sesame seeds into the sauce. Allow the sauce to cool to room temperature. Use immediately or refrigerate in a covered container for up to 2 weeks.

FORK OF MICROGREENS
WITH ALMOND VINAIGRETTE
AND ROQUEFORT

serves 6

This is a one-bite eruption on the end of a fork, although, if you prefer, you can serve this diminutive salad on a plate and lay a fork next to it. Microgreens are tender yet intense little specialty greens, which, because they are trendy, are quite accessible.

I buy microgreens and other produce from an amazing farmer we call Farmer Jones. His real name is Lee Jones and he owns Chef's Garden, a beautiful farm in Huron, Ohio, where he has done more for connecting farms and restaurants than anyone I know in the country. I particularly like celery greens and beet greens, and for this salad, my first choice is celery microgreens.

Search out the very best Roquefort cheese you can. It's sheep's milk cheese made in the south of France, where it's aged in limestone caverns—long ago discovered to be the ideal environment for the cheese's characteristic green-gray mold to develop. Authentic Roquefort bears a red seal, and all these cheeses are good. Taste a number to decide which is your favorite—not an unpleasant task! This amuse is also good made with top-grade Gorgonzola or any blue cheese you particularly like. If you don't like blue cheese, use goat cheese.

1 cup mixed microgreens, such as arugula, purple kohlrabi, and tatsoi	About 2 tablespoons Almond Vinaigrette (page 245), plus more as needed
¼ cup crumbled Roquefort cheese	Salt and freshly ground black pepper

1. Combine the mixed greens and Roquefort in a medium-sized bowl. Toss with as much of the almond vinaigrette as needed to lightly coat the greens. Season to taste with salt and pepper.

2. To serve, divide the salad into 6 equal portions and place each on a decorative fork. Lay a fork on a small plate and drizzle a little vinaigrette next to the fork. Repeat to make 5 more servings.

TRUFFLED LENTIL SPOON
WITH BACON VINAIGRETTE

serves 6

Here's an easy take on saucisson, *the French classic that combines lentils and sausage, although I have chosen to serve it without the sausage. I had the best* saucisson *of my life at Paul Bocuse's restaurant in Lyon, France. I had planned to eat there one Saturday night, assured when I called ahead that the chef would be in the restaurant. I was heartbroken when I arrived to find he was not on the premises. The maître d' invited me to come back the next day so that I could get my book and menus autographed, and surprised me the next afternoon when he told me I was expected in the kitchen as the chef's guest. There, I sat at a granite table where I ate* saucisson *with Chef Bocuse himself! This truly was one of the highlights of my career, to sit and listen to the wisdom of such a legend.*

If you want to add sausage, cut a warmed link into coins and impale them on the end of the fork's tines. Lentils are legumes that cook quickly without presoaking, which makes them endlessly versatile. They are smaller and flatter than other legumes and may be yellow, brown, black, green, or mottled. The small green French lentils known as Le Puy are considered to be the finest example.

¼ cup warm cooked orange lentils (see Note)	Salt and freshly ground black pepper
¼ cup warm cooked black lentils	3 tablespoons Bacon Vinaigrette (page 245)
¼ cup warm cooked French green lentils	6 sprigs fresh chervil or flat-leaf parsley, for garnishing
3 tablespoons Truffle Vinaigrette (page 244)	

1. Combine the lentils in a medium-sized bowl and toss gently with the truffle vinaigrette. Season to taste with salt and pepper.

2. To serve, spoon about 2 tablespoons of the truffled lentils onto a decorative spoon, such as a long-handled iced tea spoon. Set the spoon on a small plate and drizzle the bacon vinaigrette over and around the "truffles." Garnish each with a sprig of chervil. Repeat to make 5 more servings.

NOTE: You can cook the lentils ahead of time and refrigerate them for up to 24 hours. Reheat them gently in a saucepan with a little water, or in the microwave, until warm. Take care not to cook them any further. You want only to warm them.

BEEF TARTARE SPOON WITH
QUAIL EGGS ON BRIOCHE

serves 6

I serve this supercute amuse on little demitasse or dessert spoons. You might have run across similar appealing little spoons in antique stores or at flea markets and fallen in love with them, but haven't been quite sure what to do with them. Here's your chance to show off your collection. No need for the spoons to match; it's almost more interesting if they don't. The beef tartare, buttery brioche, and tiny quail eggs are far more elegant than the corned beef hash, white toast, and fried eggs that inspired me to create this. But that's the idea. If you want to serve quail eggs on brioche and leave out the beef tartare, go right ahead. Called one-eyed Susans, these eggs on toast were put on the culinary map by the late chef Jean-Louis Paladin, who is missed by all of us.

Six ½-inch-thick slices brioche, homemade (page 248) or from a good bakery	6 quail eggs
1 tablespoon unsalted butter	About 1 cup Beef Tartare (recipe follows)

1. Using a 1-inch round cookie cutter, stamp out a round from each slice. Discard the bread centers or reserve them for another use. Lightly toast the bread after you cut it to keep it from crumbling.

2. Melt the butter in a small nonstick skillet or sauté pan over medium-low heat. Put the bread in the skillet.

3. One at a time, break the eggs into a small cup and slide each one into the hole in the bread. Alternatively, crack the eggs directly into the holes in the bread, but cracking them first into a cup means less breakage. Cook for 1 to 2 minutes or until the whites are set and the yolks are still runny.

4. To serve, use a slotted spatula to transfer the bread and eggs to 6 small plates. Divide the beef tartare into 6 equal portions and form into oval quenelles. Put each quenelle on a demitasse or dessert spoon. Place each filled spoon alongside each serving of quail egg on toast.

makes about 1 cup

6 ounces beef tenderloin, chilled and then cut into *brunoise* or very small dice	1 teaspoon Dijon mustard
	1 teaspoon finely chopped flat-leaf parsley
1 large egg yolk	½ teaspoon grated orange zest
4 teaspoons drained capers, chopped	¼ teaspoon Worcestershire sauce
	Tabasco or other hot pepper sauce
1½ tablespoons finely chopped shallots	Salt and freshly ground black pepper

1. Put the beef, egg yolk, capers, shallots, mustard, parsley, zest, and Worcestershire sauce in a small bowl. Stir until well mixed. Season to taste with Tabasco, salt, and pepper.

2. Cover with plastic wrap and refrigerate (for up to 2 hours) until ready to serve.

juice*amuse*

To juice fruits and vegetables, you need a juicer. This is a powerful machine that actually extracts juice from the produce—pure juice without any body. These are not the same appliances that help you squeeze pulpy juice from citrus fruit. These machines are strong enough to get juice from apples, carrots, and beets.

While you don't need to buy the most expensive juicer on the market, I suggest you purchase a reliable one. It will last for years, and as you become used to juicing, you'll use it often. Look for a machine that is easy to use and easy to clean. The pulp accumulates in a strainer, which has to be cleaned after every use.

The amount of juice you will get from any fruit or vegetable depends on its moisture content, when and where it was harvested, and how it was stored. For this reason, it's always advisable to buy more produce than you will actually need.

Wash the fruits and vegetables before juicing them. Cut off any soft or obvious brown spots and scrub them with a soft pad if they seem to need it. Cut them into sizes small enough to go through the juicer's feed tube, but don't worry about peeling them or removing stems or small seeds. (Peel citrus fruits, however, to avoid bitterness.) The juicer extracts the liquid from the fruit or vegetable and separates the pulp (skin, seeds, stems, and all). The juice is exceptionally clear and pure. The pulp is not good for much, but it's great for composting.

JUICING CHART

makes about 3/4 cup of juice

- Apples: 1 pound
- Asparagus: 1 pound
- Beets: 12 ounces
- Blood oranges: 3 large fruit
- Cantaloupe: 1 pound
- Carrots: 1 pound
- Celery: 12 ounces
- Corn kernels: 1 pound

- Cucumbers: 12 ounces
- Fennel: 12 ounces
- Grapefruit: 1 pound
- Honeydew melon: 1 pound
- Pears: 1 pound
- Watermelon: 1 pound
- Yukon Gold potatoes: 18 ounces

PASSION FRUIT JUICE

WITH LEMON BALM

serves 6; makes about 2 cups

The first time I tasted passion fruit was at the restaurant in the Strathallen Hotel in Rochester, New York—the kitchen where I began my culinary training in 1980. There, one of my mentors, Chef Greg Broman, made passion fruit-flavored butter to serve with boiled lobster. It was amazing! Later, I developed a recipe for lobster salad with a passion fruit vinaigrette, and the fruit quickly became one of my all-time favorites. When I started making juices, I tried passion fruit juice and discovered that a little lemon balm deepens its already full-bodied flavor. Unless you have access to passion fruit, use passion fruit puree, which is usually easier to find than the fruit, although you might have to buy it frozen.

¼ cup passion fruit puree	About ¼ cup Simple Syrup
2 bunches fresh lemon balm	(page 251)
1 cup water	1 tablespoon fresh orange juice
	Salt and freshly ground black pepper

1. Put the passion fruit puree, the lemon balm, and ½ cup of the water in a large saucepan and bring to a simmer over medium-high heat. As soon as the mixture simmers, remove it from the heat and allow to steep for 20 minutes.

2. Strain through a *chinois* or fine-mesh sieve into a large pitcher. Stir in the remaining ½ cup water. Add the syrup to taste and the orange juice. Allow to cool to room temperature. Cover and refrigerate for at least 2 hours or until chilled. Season to taste with salt and pepper.

3. Stir before pouring into small, chilled glasses for serving.

HONEYDEW MELON JUICE
WITH PINK PEPPERCORNS

---

serves 6; makes about 2 cups

My six-year-old son, Gio, is the world's biggest melon fan. He eats it almost every day for breakfast, although he prefers watermelon and "orange melon" to "green melon." Still, when he eats green honeydew, he greedily drinks the juice in the bottom of the bowl, which got me started experimenting with melon juices. I tried a number of variations but finally came up with this simple mixture of honeydew juice and pink peppercorns. The peppercorns cut through the melon's sweetness, and when you strain the juice, pleasing pale-pink streaks remain in the refreshing juice.

2 cups honeydew melon juice (see page 184)	1 tablespoon fresh lime juice
1 tablespoon pink peppercorns	Salt and freshly ground black pepper

1. Strain the melon juice through a *chinois* or fine-mesh sieve into a bowl.

2. Spread the pink peppercorns in a small dry skillet and toast over medium-high heat for 40 to 50 seconds or until they are fragrant. Transfer to a plate to stop cooking and allow to cool completely.

3. Stir the cooled peppercorns and the lime juice into the melon juice and set aside for 30 minutes to allow the flavors to develop.

4. Strain through a *chinois* or fine-mesh sieve lined with cheesecloth into a large pitcher. Cover and refrigerate for 2 hours or until chilled. Season to taste with salt and pepper.

5. Stir before pouring into small, chilled glasses for serving.

CELERY-PEAR JUICE

serves 6 ; makes about 2 cups

By now you may have gathered that I am especially fond of celery. I love its clean freshness. At Tru, I serve celery puree with light fish such as halibut and cod, and then spoon caramelized pears on top. This juice is an outgrowth of those flavors. The first time I juiced pears and celery, I was hooked. I sometimes whisk this juice with olive oil for a vinaigrette and serve it with grilled fish. Different pears will vary the flavor, and while I use all varieties as their fall season progresses, I am comfortable with any, such as Bartlett, Anjou, or Comice. Some are sweeter and more floral than others.

1 pound Bartlett pears, cored	2 cups celery juice (see page 184)
One 1½-inch cinnamon stick	1 tablespoon fresh lemon juice
1 small bunch fresh thyme	Salt and freshly ground white pepper

1. Juice the pears in a juicer (see page 184). Skim and remove any foam from the surface of the juice. Transfer the juice to a small saucepan and add the cinnamon and thyme and bring to a simmer over medium-high heat. As soon as the juice simmers, remove it from the heat and allow to steep for 10 minutes. Skim and remove any foam that rises to the surface.

2. Strain the pear juice through a paper coffee filter into a large pitcher and allow to come to room temperature.

3. Strain the celery juice through a *chinois* or fine-mesh sieve into the pitcher with the pear juice. Add the lemon juice, stir to mix, cover, and refrigerate for at least 2 hours or until chilled. Season to taste with salt and white pepper.

4. Stir before pouring into small, chilled glasses for serving.

CUCUMBER JUICE

WITH PINEAPPLE MINT

serves 6; makes about 2 cups

When I made cold cucumber soup one summer, I juiced some extra cucumbers to punch up the soup's flavor. As I worked, I drank nearly as much of the juice as I stirred into the soup, which led me to believe my customers would like it too. I experimented to find an herb that would best complement the cucumbers, and while both sage and basil were good, the mints tasted best. I suggest you experiment on your own with the fresh mints and basils available nowadays. Serve this icy cold—it will quench any thirst!

2 cups water

1 bunch fresh pineapple mint

2 cups cucumber juice (see page 184)

1 tablespoon fresh lemon juice

About 1 cup Simple Syrup (page 251)

Salt and freshly ground black pepper

1. Put the water and pineapple mint in a medium-sized saucepan and bring to a simmer over medium-high heat. Reduce the heat and simmer very gently for 5 minutes. Remove from the heat and set aside to steep until the water comes to room temperature.

2. Strain through a *chinois* or fine-mesh sieve into a bowl.

3. Strain the cucumber juice through a *chinois* or fine-mesh sieve into a large pitcher. Stir in the infused water. Add the lemon juice and enough of the syrup to balance any bitterness. Season to taste with salt and pepper. Cover and refrigerate for 2 hours or until chilled.

4. Stir before pouring into small, chilled glasses for serving.

WATERMELON JUICE

WITH LEMON VERBENA

serves 6; makes about 3 cups

Just a few fresh leaves of lemon verbena steeped in water add a lovely, deepening dimension to this juice. But, best of all, a chilly sip of this refreshing drink instantly takes you back to those hot summer days when nothing quenched your thirst better than a slice of frigid watermelon. Watermelon may be red, pink, or yellow, with or without seeds, but regardless of these minor differences, juice made from watermelon tastes exhilaratingly sweet. You need to try it. It's one of my favorites and if you don't try it, you're missing out on one of the best juices you can make. Garnish it with chunks of watermelon of another color: for example, pink juice with yellow watermelon and vice versa, or scatter the shiny black pits over the plate for decoration. But however you serve it, make sure it's ice-cold.

1 cup water

10 fresh lemon verbena leaves

2 cups watermelon juice (see page 184)

1 tablespoon fresh lime juice

Salt and freshly ground black pepper

1. Put the water and lemon verbena leaves in a saucepan and bring to a simmer over medium-high heat. As soon as the mixture simmers, remove it from the heat and allow to steep for 15 minutes.

2. Strain through a *chinois* or fine-mesh sieve into a large pitcher and allow to come to room temperature.

3. Strain the watermelon juice through a *chinois* or fine-mesh sieve into the pitcher of lemon verbena–infused water and stir. Stir in the lime juice. Season to taste with salt and pepper. Cover and refrigerate for at least 2 hours or until chilled.

4. Stir before pouring into small, chilled glasses for serving.

WHITE PEACH JUICE
WITH TARRAGON

serves 6; makes about 1¹/₂ cups

While you can make seductively sweet juice with any perfectly ripe peach, white peaches have a special allure for many people. This is particularly true of my culinary partner, Gale Gand, who is crazy about them. Gale, who bakes with them whenever she can, introduced me to them very early in our relationship. Serving white peach juice as an amuse *was inspired by her, and the addition of fresh tarragon, which kicks up the flavor of the peaches with a tinge of licorice, makes this a great favorite in the restaurant. Be sure the peaches—white or yellow—are very ripe; almost overripe peaches are best.*

5 ripe white peaches, pits removed

2 sprigs fresh tarragon

1 tablespoon fresh lemon juice

Salt and freshly ground white pepper

1. Juice the peaches in a juicer (see page 184).
2. Strain the juice through a *chinois* or fine-mesh sieve into a small saucepan. Add the tarragon and bring to a simmer over medium-high heat. Reduce the heat and simmer gently for 10 minutes.
3. Strain through a *chinois* or fine-mesh sieve into a pitcher. Stir in the lemon juice. Allow to cool to room temperature. Cover and refrigerate for 2 hours or until chilled. Season to taste with salt and white pepper.
4. Stir before pouring into small, chilled glasses for serving.

POMEGRANATE JUICE

WITH CLOVES

serves 6; makes about 1 1/2 cups

When you decide to make pomegranate juice, prepare yourself for a big mess—and a joyful treat. No matter how careful you are, when you dig the tiny juice-filled seeds from the fruit and then crush them, some of the bright-red liquid will spray on the work surface and stain your fingers. Never mind. The mess is part of the fun. The cloves add a pinch of spiciness that complements the sweet-sour pomegranate juice.

Large, heavy, deep-red pomegranates are best. The heft signifies lots of seeds buried in the white parched membrane. The tough outer skin should be thin enough so that you can feel and practically see the pulpy seeds bursting through it. Break the fruit along scored lines, as the recipe instructs. Cutting through the skin with a knife breaks the seeds. I love thinking about how the fruit has been enjoyed since biblical times and has long been an important food in the Middle East.

7 pomegranates	About 6 tablespoons Simple Syrup
2 whole cloves	(page 251)
1 tablespoon fresh lime juice	Salt and freshly ground black pepper

1. Using a serrated knife, slice the knobs from the base of the pomegranates. Score each fruit lengthwise into quarters. Gently break apart the fruit along the scored lines. Scoop out the seed clusters and crush them in a small bowl with the back of a spoon or your hands.

2. Put the crushed fruit, along with any accumulated juices, in a fine-mesh sieve set over a small saucepan. Press down on the fruit to extract as much juice as possible.

3. Put the cloves in a small, dry skillet and toast over medium-high heat for 30 to 40 seconds or until fragrant.

4. Add the cloves to the saucepan containing the juice and bring to a simmer over medium-high heat. Reduce the heat and simmer gently for 5 minutes. Remove from the heat and set aside to steep until the juice cools to room temperature.

5. Strain through a *chinois* or fine-mesh sieve into a pitcher. Add the lime juice and enough of the syrup to balance any bitterness. Cover and refrigerate for 2 hours or until chilled. Season to taste with salt and pepper.

6. Stir before pouring into small, chilled glasses for serving.

RUBY RED GRAPEFRUIT JUICE
WITH RED BEET JUICE

serves 6; makes about 1¹⁄₂ cups

I grew up avoiding grapefruit at all costs. I could not tolerate that much sourness first thing in the morning, even when my mother sprinkled it liberally with sugar. When I worked at the Stapleford Park Hotel in Leicestershire, England, Malcolm, the gamekeeper, who knew my love of food, repeatedly urged me to try one of the grapefruit he brought to work almost daily when he brought me braces of hares and pheasant. (He also took me hunting in Scotland, where we found time to travel the "whiskey trail," visiting the various distillers of Scotch whiskey. My education was complete!) I finally gave in to the grapefruit and wondered why I had been resistant for so many years! I joyfully ate grapefruit daily after that. When I began juicing, I juiced gorgeous Israeli Red grapefruit and Ruby Red grapefruit and sweetened the juice with a little beet juice. I don't stir in the beet juice but instead drop little spoonfuls into the glasses so that it floats on top, kind of a lava lamp effect. It's really pretty.

3 or 4 Ruby Red or California Oroblanco grapefruit, peeled (about 1¹⁄₂ pounds)	Salt and freshly ground black pepper 1 tablespoon fresh lime juice 1 red beet

1. Juice 3 grapefruit in a juicer (see page 184). Measure the juice. There should be about 1¹⁄₂ cups. If you don't have enough, peel and juice another grapefruit and add its juice to measure a total of 1¹⁄₂ cups of juice.

2. Strain the juice through a *chinois* or fine-mesh sieve into a pitcher and stir in the lime juice. Season to taste with salt and pepper. Cover and refrigerate for 2 hours or until chilled.

3. Juice the beet in the juicer. Strain the juice through a *chinois* or fine-mesh sieve into a small bowl and then pour into a squeeze bottle. Cover and refrigerate for 2 hours or until chilled. Season to taste with salt and pepper.

4. Stir the grapefruit juice before pouring into small, chilled glasses for serving. Garnish with drops of beet juice.

CARROT JUICE

WITH GINGER SYRUP

serves 6; makes about 4 cups

When I was looking for a light shooter to serve as an early-fall amuse, I began thinking about tomato water and cucumber juice. It turned out that both were too light. Around this time, I visited several juice bars, which were popping up all over Chicago, and was blown away by the carrot juice—it tasted so fresh, rich, and satisfying. While I love fruit juices, I keep coming back to carrot juice with its deep color and pure flavor. I juice white, red, orange, and purple carrots and all taste good, although each is slightly different. No matter what kind of carrot, the flavor holds and the color looks great in a stubby shot glass. Ginger is a natural with the carrots in this juice, since the two flavors are a marriage anyone can sanction.

¼ cup water

¼ cup sugar

One 1-inch piece fresh ginger, peeled
    and sliced

Salt and freshly ground black pepper

2½ pounds carrots

1 tablespoon fresh lemon juice

1. In a small heavy saucepan, heat the water and sugar over medium-high heat, stirring until boiling. Let the syrup cook for a few minutes until the sugar dissolves and the syrup looks clear.

2. Add the ginger and bring the syrup back to a boil. Cook for 1 to 2 minutes.

3. Remove from the heat and allow to cool slightly. Transfer the syrup to a glass container, cover, and set aside at room temperature to cool. Cover and refrigerate for at least 6 hours until chilled. Season to taste with salt and pepper.

4. Before using, strain the ginger from the syrup through a fine-mesh sieve.

5. Juice the carrots in a juicer (see page 184). Strain the juice through a *chinois* or fine-mesh sieve into a large pitcher.

6. Stir the syrup and lemon juice into the carrot juice and season with salt before pouring into small, chilled glasses for serving.

BLOOD ORANGE JUICE

WITH THAI BASIL

s e r v e s   6 ;   m a k e s   a b o u t   1½   c u p s

I recall the three weeks I spent in Italy during blood orange season when I eagerly drank the crimson juice flavored with basil every morning. I tried it with Thai basil, purple basil—any basil, for that matter. The juice is a clean-tasting palate starter. Blood oranges are originally from Sicily but are now grown in other parts of Italy and in Spain. I put them through a juicer, but if you prefer, squeeze them as you would any oranges and then strain them for a delicate-tasting, boldly hued elixir. This should be ice-cold, so don't let the juice sit out for any length of time.

3 blood oranges, peeled, plus more as needed	About ¼ cup Simple Syrup (page 251)
10 fresh Thai basil leaves	Salt and freshly ground black pepper
1 tablespoon fresh lemon juice	

1. Juice the blood oranges in a juicer (see page 184). Measure the juice. There should be about 1½ cups. Peel and juice additional blood oranges, as needed, to measure a total of 1½ cups of juice.

2. Strain through a *chinois* or fine-mesh sieve into a small saucepan. Add the basil and bring to a simmer over medium-high heat. Reduce the heat and simmer gently for 5 minutes. Remove from the heat and set aside to steep until the juice comes to room temperature.

3. Strain again through a *chinois* or fine-mesh sieve into a pitcher. Add the lemon juice and enough of the syrup to balance any bitterness. Cover and refrigerate for 2 hours or until chilled. Season to taste with salt and pepper.

4. Stir before pouring into small, chilled glasses for serving.

serves 6; makes about 1½ cups

Not everyone thinks of juicing tangerines or any of their close relatives such as clementines, satsumas, temple oranges, tangelos, and Minneolas, but all make really good, intensely flavored citrus juices. Tangerines, which should more authentically be called mandarin oranges, are easy to peel and section, which makes them and their cousins naturals for eating out of hand. But don't stop there. Juice them! I add a little sage to boost the overall impact of the juice, but if you can't find fresh sage, don't use dried. It's better to leave it out altogether.

4 tangerines	About 6 tablespoons Simple Syrup
3 large fresh sage leaves	(page 251)
1 tablespoon fresh lime juice	Salt and freshly ground black pepper

1. Juice the tangerines in a juicer (see page 184). Strain the juice through a *chinois* or fine-mesh sieve into a small saucepan. Add the sage and bring to a simmer over medium-high heat. Reduce the heat and simmer gently for 5 minutes. Remove from the heat and set aside to steep until the juice cools to room temperature.

2. Strain again through a *chinois* or fine-mesh sieve into a pitcher. Add the lime juice and enough of the syrup to balance any bitterness. Cover and refrigerate for 2 hours or until chilled. Season to taste with salt and pepper.

3. Stir before pouring into small, chilled glasses for serving.

APPLE-ROSEMARY JUICE

serves 6; makes about 3 cups

If I were going to bottle anything for commercial sale, this would be it. Not only is this juice my personal favorite, but discovering how a little rosemary rounds out apple juice so that it is cleanly refreshing as well as complex was a glorious surprise. The juice is practically clear, so the first sip is an intense revelation—your guests will be delighted! For a tint of color, add a little green or red apple peel to the simmering juice. Coming to a store near you soon!

½ cup fresh lemon juice	3 sprigs fresh rosemary
2 cups water	Salt and freshly ground black pepper
1 pound firm, tart apples (3 or 4 apples), such as Braeburn, Gala, or Granny Smith	

1. Combine the lemon juice and water in a small nonreactive bowl. Core and quarter the apples and place in the acidulated water.
2. Juice as many of the apple quarters as needed in a juicer (see page 184) to measure 2 cups. Skim any foam or impurities from the surface of the juice and discard. Transfer the juice to a small saucepan. Add the rosemary and bring to a simmer over medium-high heat. As soon as the juice simmers, remove from the heat and allow to steep for 1 hour.
3. Skim and discard any foam from the surface of the mixture.
4. Strain through a coffee filter into a large pitcher and allow the juice to come to room temperature. Cover and refrigerate for 2 hours or until chilled. Season to taste with salt and pepper.
5. Stir before pouring into small, chilled glasses for serving.

foam

I owe my fascination and success with foams to Ferran Adria, who is the chef-owner of the world-renowned three-star Michelin restaurant El Bulli, in Barcelona. Not only is he responsible for creating foams, but he introduced them to the restaurant world. Several years ago, I discovered that my friend Chef Jose Andres, from Washington, D.C., had been one of Chef Adria's sous-chefs in Spain, and I immediately prevailed upon him to travel to Spain with me and introduce us. Today, I proudly call Ferran Adria my friend, one whom I admire greatly.

When I spent time with Chef Adria, eating and studying his philosophy in his kitchen and laboratory in Barcelona, I realized his approach is like no other. For instance, one night I was his guest at the kitchen table in his restaurant, where he made fettuccini carbonara with sheets of gelatin instead of pasta. If you closed your eyes, you'd never guess it was not pasta, but it was a flavor spoof that was at once technical and cerebral. He followed this dish with forty more courses (or "tastes"), cooking each one in the order of when he created it. Those five hours probably constitute the most amazing experience of my culinary life. El Bulli is open for about six months a year, and the chef takes the other six months to experiment with flavors, textures, and techniques. He likes nothing more than educating other chefs and is incredibly generous with his knowledge. Thank you, Ferran!

Foams are great for amuse-bouche and hors d'oeuvres, particularly when you're having a cocktail party or sizable dinner party. Just place a little mound on a crispy toast or cracker, sliced cucumber, potato chip, or oyster in its shell. What could be easier?

When I make a foam, I find that it's best to make a sizable quantity. I have found that if you start with less than half a canister, the foams aren't great. But this should not be a problem; I have stored foams in the canister in the refrigerator for up to a week, depending on what they are. Obviously, those made with fish and seafood are less stable than those made with cheese or potatoes.

ISI canisters and their CO_2 cartridges are sold at fine kitchen stores such as Williams-Sonoma and Sur la Table. The large ones available for home use hold up to 6 cups of liquid and yield 10 cups of foam. The smaller ones hold up to 3 cups and yield 5 cups of foam. For the recipes here, I recommend using the smaller canisters.

At Tru, we have found that we get the best results with half-filled canisters. The following recipes, which use the smaller canisters, usually need only one cartridge, but if the foam does not foam satisfactorily, just add another cartridge. For the 4 to 5 cups that these recipes yield, I begin with 1 ½ to 2 cups of liquid.

Follow the recipe instructions about chilling the canister both before and after it is filled. The colder, the better. At the restaurant, we hold the canisters on ice for about an hour before we spray the foam from them.

ARTICHOKE BARIGOULE

WITH GOAT CHEESE FOAM

....

serves 6

Artichokes and goat cheese are a perfect match, so when I decided to transform this flavor combination into a one-bite amuse, *I naturally gravitated toward the idea of a goat cheese* spuma, *or foam. Since chilling food always dulls its taste, I first simmer the tender artichoke hearts in wine with classic mirepoix ingredients to enhance the artichokes' flavor. The goat cheese foam tastes distinctively yet subtly of goat cheese, and never overwhelms the thin slices of artichoke.*

Goat cheese just gets more and more popular, which is good news for cheese lovers. I have spent time with some wonderful American goat cheese makers such as Laurie Chenel in northern California, Susi Cahn of Coach Dairy Goat Farms in New York State, and Judy Shad in Indiana. All three women make excellent artisanal cheeses that appeal to the American palate—cheeses that are soft, mild, smooth, and subtle. But they are not the only cheese makers around. Keep an eye out for local goat cheese makers who might be offering their product at farmers' markets.

1½ teaspoons fresh lemon juice	½ tablespoon salt
5 artichoke hearts (see Note)	About ¾ cup dry white wine
¼ cup olive oil	4 ounces soft goat cheese, at room
1 cup finely chopped onions	temperature
½ cup finely chopped celery	1¾ cups chilled heavy cream
½ cup finely chopped carrots	Freshly ground black pepper

1. Fill a large glass, ceramic, or other nonreactive bowl with water and add the lemon juice. Drop the artichoke hearts into the water.

2. Heat the olive oil in a large saucepan over low heat. Add the onions, celery, and carrots and cook slowly, stirring frequently, for about 10 minutes or until the vegetables are softened but not colored.

3. Drain the artichokes and add them to the pan along with the salt. Pour in as much of the wine as needed to cover the artichokes completely. Bring to a boil over medium-high heat. Reduce the heat and simmer for 30 to 40 minutes or until the artichokes are tender. Re-

move the artichoke hearts from the pan and allow them to cool on a plate. When cool, slice into sections about 1¼ inches thick. Refrigerate until cold.

4. Put the goat cheese in a small bowl and mash gently with the back of a fork or spoon. Slowly mix in the cream. When the cheese is smooth and the cream completely incorporated, season to taste with salt and pepper.

5. Strain the goat cheese through a *chinois* or fine-mesh sieve into another bowl and then pour into the chilled canister of a foamer. The amount will fill it about halfway. Charge with 1 or 2 charges. Chill for at least 1 hour before serving.

6. To serve, arrange some artichoke sections on a small plate. Shake the foamer vigorously and place a little of the goat cheese foam on top. Repeat to make 5 more servings. Serve chilled.

NOTE: To cut the artichoke hearts from globe artichokes, trim the stems flush with the base and cut off the pointed tops. Remove the outer leaves until only the tender ones remain. Scoop out the prickly chokes and discard. Drop the trimmed artichoke hearts into the acidulated water as they are cut. This is to prevent them from turning brown.

WASABI FOAM WITH
TUNA AND WASABI TOBIKO

---

serves 6 to 10

I love sashimi and sushi, which for me is as much about eating great raw tuna and shockingly hot wasabi—the pungent Japanese horseradish—as anything else. When the wasabi powder is mixed with heavy cream and a bit of honey and then aerated into a foam, it's unbelievably luxurious with the thinly sliced tuna. The wasabi "caviar" looks like bright-green speckles on the plate. It's nothing more exotic than tobiko, or flying fish roe, cured in wasabi horseradish so that it turns green and absorbs great flavor, and is sold in some Asian markets.

Unlike the familiar white horseradish, the wasabi horseradish root is green. It has thicker bark than white horseradish, which when peeled reveals green fibers. It's sold in Japanese and Asian markets, very often alongside sharkskin graters. Buy one of these, too. When you grate fresh wasabi on them, the fibers dissolve into a juicy, wet paste, just as you want it.

¼ cup wasabi powder	Salt
2 cups chilled heavy cream	½ pound sushi-quality tuna
1 tablespoon honey	2 ounces wasabi *tobiko*

1. Put the wasabi powder in a medium-sized bowl. Slowly pour in the heavy cream and whisk until the mixture is very smooth. Whisk in the honey and season to taste with salt. Set aside for 10 minutes to allow the flavors to develop.

2. Pour the wasabi cream into the chilled canister of a foamer. The amount will fill it about halfway. Charge with 1 or 2 charges. Chill for at least 1 hour before serving.

3. To serve, slice the tuna as thinly as possible and place on small plates. Season to taste with salt. Shake the foamer vigorously and place a little of the wasabi foam on each plate, next to the tuna. Garnish each serving with wasabi *tobiko*.

GREEN-LIPPED MUSSELS WITH SPICY POTATO SALAD AND HORSERADISH FOAM

serves 6 to 10

Because I love potato salad and horseradish, and because mussels are a wonderful summertime food, I decided to put them together. I thought about using the horseradish in a vinaigrette, sauce, or mayonnaise, but none of those seemed exactly right. Finally, I tried it as a foam and it was great! The creaminess and lightness of the foam cuts through the horseradish without nullifying it. Spoon a little potato salad into a mussel shell, top it with a plump, steamed mussel, and finish with a dollop of foam—outstanding!

When I can, I serve green-lipped mussels for this amuse, which I remember eating in New Zealand with great fondness. Years ago, when I was still with Trio, the owner of an Auckland restaurant called Cin Cin on Quay walked into my kitchen and offered me the opportunity to spend three weeks in New Zealand as a guest chef. When the plane tickets arrived, I was there! After ten days of cooking, and training the Cin Cin staff, I spent the remainder of the visit touring the gorgeous countryside, and happily accepted an invitation to join a mussel farming boat for a day. The boat was more like a tanker than a fishing boat and we headed out to the massive green-lipped mussel farms in the middle of the ocean. The crew hauled from the depths huge ropes thick with mussels. Large burlap sacks filled with mussels were transported from the boat's deck back to shore by helicopter. On board, we slurped raw mussels from shells still dripping with seawater, and we steamed still more. From the ocean to the pot to our mouths. It doesn't get much better.

2 cups grated fresh horseradish

2 teaspoons Worcestershire sauce

2 cups chilled heavy cream

Salt and freshly ground white pepper

½ pound green-lipped or other black or green mussels, rinsed and scrubbed

½ cup dry white wine

1 shallot, finely sliced

1 bunch fresh thyme, plus more for garnishing

Spicy Potato Salad (recipe follows)

Kosher or coarse salt (optional)

1. Put the grated horseradish, Worcestershire sauce, and heavy cream into a large bowl and set aside for 15 to 20 minutes to allow the horseradish to infuse the cream. Whisk until blended. Season to taste with salt and white pepper.

2. Strain through a *chinois* or fine-mesh sieve into another large bowl.

3. Pour the horseradish cream into the chilled canister of a foamer. The amount will fill it about halfway. Charge with 1 or 2 charges. Chill for at least 1 hour before serving.

4. Put the mussels in a saucepan with the white wine, shallot, and thyme sprigs. Cover and steam over high heat, shaking the pan occasionally, for 3 to 5 minutes or until the mussels have opened. Remove from the heat. Discard any unopened mussels. Remove the mussels from the liquid, transfer to a shallow bowl, cover, and chill thoroughly.

5. Remove the mussels from their shells, reserving the bottom shells for presentation. Discard the top shells.

6. To serve, fill the reserved bottom shells with potato salad and top with a mussel. Shake the foamer vigorously and place a little horseradish foam alongside each mussel. Garnish the mussel with a thyme sprig. Arrange each filled shell on a small plate. Alternatively, put coarse salt in a small bowl and add enough water to mix the salt to the texture of sand. Pile some "sand" on the plate and set the shell on top.

SPICY POTATO SALAD

serves 6 to 10

5 small red-skinned potatoes (about 7 ounces), unpeeled, scrubbed, and rinsed	1 tablespoon finely snipped chives
	2 tablespoons mayonnaise
Salt	Freshly ground black pepper
1 shallot, finely minced	Cayenne pepper

1. Cut the potatoes into very small dice and put in a medium-sized saucepan. Add enough cold water to cover and then lightly salt the water. Bring to a boil over medium-high heat. Reduce the heat and simmer for about 5 minutes or until just tender. Drain and immediately submerge in cold water. Drain again.

2. Toss the potatoes, shallot, and chives in a bowl. Add the mayonnaise and mix gently until the vegetables are coated. Season to taste with salt, pepper, and cayenne.

SQUASH BLOSSOMS
WITH BASIL FOAM

serves 6 to 10

This is an especially pretty amuse. *An obvious summer dish, it's surprisingly easy to make when squash blossoms are available and you can get the very best fresh basil. Years ago, my longtime friend Todd English, chef-owner of the nationally renowned restaurants Olives and Figs, stopped at Brasserie T, the restaurant I then owned, while on tour for his first book. He prepared a lovely tomato-basil salad with fried squash blossoms that impressed me sufficiently that I remembered the flavor combinations when I developed this* amuse.

2 ½ sheets gelatin	1 cup heavy cream
About 8 ounces fresh basil, stems removed	Salt and freshly ground black pepper
1 cup half-and-half	6 to 10 large squash blossoms

1. Fill a large bowl with cold water. Gently drop the gelatin sheets into the water until submerged. Let soften and bloom for about 5 minutes.

2. In a saucepan filled with boiling water, blanch the basil leaves for a few seconds. Drain and immediately submerge in cold water. Drain again.

3. Put the drained basil, with some water still clinging to the leaves, in a blender and puree until nearly smooth.

4. Put the half-and-half and heavy cream in a large saucepan and bring to a boil over medium-high heat. As soon as the cream boils, remove from the heat.

5. Using your hands, lift the gelatin sheets from the water and squeeze them gently between your fingers. Transfer the sheets to the hot cream. Stir gently until dissolved. Stir in the pureed basil. Strain through a *chinois* or fine-mesh sieve into a large bowl. Season to taste with salt and pepper and set aside to cool to room temperature.

6. Pour the basil mixture into the chilled canister of a foamer. The amount will fill it about halfway. Charge with 1 or 2 charges. Chill for at least 1 hour before serving.

7. To serve, cut a slice off the stem end of each squash blossom so that the opening is about the size of a quarter. Shake the foamer vigorously and fill each blossom completely with basil foam. Arrange the blossoms on 6 to 10 small plates.

VANILLA FOAM WITH
FINGERLING POTATO CHIPS

serves 6

When customers at Tru take their first taste of this, their reaction is: "Wow! What is it?" And then they are amazed to hear it's a potato foam flavored with vanilla, of all things. I think the combination is as magical as it is surprising.

6 to 8 all-purpose potatoes (about 2 pounds), peeled and chopped	1 sheet gelatin
	Vegetable oil
3 vanilla beans	1 to 2 fingerling potatoes, unpeeled
Salt	Kosher or coarse salt, for garnishing
1 cup cold water	Finely chopped fresh mint, for garnishing

1. Put the all-purpose potatoes in a large saucepan and add enough cold water to cover by at least 3 inches. Bring to a boil over high heat. Reduce the heat and simmer for about 15 minutes or until tender when pierced with a fork. Drain.

2. Pass the potatoes through a food mill and put in a large bowl. Split the vanilla beans and scrape the seeds into the potatoes and stir to mix. Season to taste with salt.

3. Put the water in a small saucepan. Gently drop the gelatin sheet into the water and let soften and bloom for about 5 minutes. Bring to a simmer over medium-high heat. Cook, stirring, for about 2 minutes or until the gelatin dissolves. Pour into the potatoes and stir to mix.

4. Strain the potato base through a *chinois* or fine-mesh sieve. Repeat 3 more times for a total of 4 passes so that the potatoes are very finely strained. Rinse the *chinois* or sieve between batches, if necessary.

5. Pour the puree into the chilled canister of a foamer. The amount will fill it about halfway. Charge with 1 or 2 charges. Chill for at least 1 hour before serving.

6. Pour the vegetable oil into a deep heavy saucepan to a depth of about 2 inches. Heat over high heat until a deep-frying thermometer registers 350°F.

7. Use a Japanese mandolin to cut the fingerling potatoes crosswise into 18 very thin slices. If you don't have a mandolin, use a small sharp knife to cut very thin slices.

8. Gently pat the potato slices with paper towels. Drop the slices into the hot oil and fry for 1 to

2 minutes or until golden brown. Remove from the oil with a slotted spoon and drain on a double thickness of paper towels. Sprinkle with salt while still hot. Transfer the chips to a wire rack to cool.

9. To serve, set 3 potato chips on a small plate. Shake the foamer vigorously and place a little vanilla foam on the chips. Garnish each with a sprinkle of kosher salt and chopped mint. Repeat to make 5 more servings.

ROASTED GARLIC FOAM

WITH BLACK OLIVE CROSTINI

serves 10

Anyone who has smeared roasted garlic on good, crusty bread, like the kind they serve in French bistros and Italian trattorias, will understand what inspired me to develop this mellow-flavored foam. The brininess of the black olives punches up the flavor profile of the amuse, slathered as it is on the little toasts and then topped with the creamy foam. Close your eyes and you're immediately transported to a sidewalk café in Paris.

4 heads garlic, unpeeled	½ cup pitted and chopped Kalamata olives
5 to 6 tablespoons olive oil	1 clove garlic, chopped
1 cup half-and-half	
1 cup heavy cream	Ten ¼-inch-thick slices bread, cut from a baguette
2 sheets gelatin	
Salt and freshly ground black pepper	5 oil-packed sun-dried tomatoes, drained and chopped

1. Preheat the oven to 350°F.

2. Cut the pointed tops off the garlic heads and drizzle 2 to 3 tablespoons of the oil over the exposed pulp. Wrap the heads securely in aluminum foil and arrange on a small baking tray. Roast for 20 to 30 minutes or until tender. Allow to cool slightly.

3. When cool enough to handle, extract the garlic cloves by gently squeezing on the bottoms of the heads. Strain through a *chinois* or fine-mesh sieve into a small bowl and set aside.

4. Put the half-and-half and heavy cream into a medium-sized saucepan. Bring to a boil over medium-high heat. As soon as the cream boils, remove it from the heat.

5. Meanwhile, fill a large bowl with cold water. Gently drop the gelatin sheets into the water until submerged. Let soften and bloom for about 5 minutes.

6. Using your hands, lift the gelatin sheets from the water and squeeze them gently between your fingers. Transfer the sheets to the cream mixture. Stir gently until dissolved. Add the roasted garlic puree to the cream and mix well. Season to taste with salt and pepper. Allow to cool to room temperature.

7. Strain the garlic-cream through a *chinois* or fine-mesh sieve into a large bowl. Pour into

the chilled canister of a foamer. The amount will fill it halfway. Charge with 1 or 2 charges. Chill for at least 1 hour before serving.

8. Put the olives and chopped garlic in a blender and puree. With the motor running, slowly add enough of the remaining 3 tablespoons oil to make a smooth paste. Transfer the olive paste to a small bowl.

9. Toast both sides of the bread under the broiler or in a toaster until golden brown.

10. To serve, spread a thin layer of the olive paste over the bread and top with tomatoes. Arrange each slice on a small plate. Shake the foamer vigorously and place a little of the roasted garlic foam on top of the *crostini*.

BLUE CHEESE FOAM WITH
PORT WINE REDUCTION

serves 6 to 8

I was inspired to make this as a spin on a salad I used to make at my restaurant Brasserie T with blue cheese, grapes, and spicy pecans. It was one of the most popular dishes we served, and you'll find the salad in my first book, American Brasserie. When I started making foams, I found blue cheese foam to be light, intensely flavored, and yet not as rich and heavy as straight blue cheese. The port reduction works nicely and makes this foam fun to serve. Always use a good port—medium to high end—for a reduction. If you wouldn't drink it, don't cook with it. Here I use dry port, but if you only have sweet port, use it.

3 cups dry port wine	5 ounces blue cheese, crumbled
2 cups chilled heavy cream	Salt and freshly ground black pepper

1. Put the port wine into a medium-sized saucepan and bring to a boil over medium-high heat. Reduce the heat and simmer for about 25 minutes or until the wine is reduced to 1 cup. Remove from the heat and allow the reduction to cool. Transfer to a covered container or a squeeze bottle and refrigerate until needed.

2. Pour the cream into a large saucepan and bring to a boil over medium-high heat. As soon as the cream boils, remove from the heat.

3. Add the blue cheese and using a handheld immersion blender, puree until smooth. Alternatively, transfer the cream and cheese to a food processor and process until smooth. Strain through a *chinois* or fine-mesh sieve into a large bowl. Season to taste with salt and pepper and set aside to cool to room temperature.

4. Pour the blue cheese mixture into the chilled canister of a foamer. The amount will fill it halfway. Charge with 1 or 2 charges. Chill for at least 2 hours before serving.

5. To serve, shake the foamer vigorously and place a little blue cheese foam on a small plate. Garnish with a drizzle of port wine reduction. If it's too thick to drizzle, let the reduction come to room temperature. Repeat to make 5 to 7 more servings.

WHITE ANCHOVY FOAM
WITH CHIVES

serves 6

Anyone who likes anchovies should seek out white anchovies, which are imported from Italy and always packed in oil. The pale-colored meaty fish are not quite as salty as dark anchovies and I want people to discover these tiny treasures from the waters off the Italian Riviera. I like them so much, I pluck them from the jar and eat them without fanfare on a piece of crusty bread—but I also love them in this foam. Four ounces of anchovies are all you need, but if you like more anchovy flavor, use five or even six ounces. Anchovies and onions are great together, which is why I serve this foam sprinkled with snipped chives. If you make this in the summer and run across purple chive blossoms, use them to garnish the plates.

4 ounces white anchovies, patted dry with paper towels	2 tablespoons white wine vinegar
¼ cup water	Salt and freshly ground black pepper
2 cups chilled heavy cream	2 tablespoons snipped chives

1. To control the strength of the anchovies, rinse them several times under cool water. Put the anchovies and the ¼ cup water in a blender and puree until smooth. Transfer to a large bowl.

2. Slowly stir in the cream until smooth. Add the vinegar and mix well. Strain through a *chinois* or fine-mesh sieve into another large bowl. Season to taste with salt and pepper.

3. Pour the cream into the chilled canister of a foamer. The amount will fill it halfway. Charge with 1 or 2 charges. Chill for at least 1 hour before serving.

4. To serve, shake the foamer vigorously and place a little white anchovy foam on a small plate. Garnish with a sprinkling of snipped chives. Repeat to make 5 more servings.

savory sorbet *amuse*

I developed a collection of savory sorbets as palate starters; they're not the traditional palate cleansers. I loved the chilled flavors of the vegetables, herbs, and spices used here and decided they were a terrific way to excite customers about the meal to come. I serve them in flavored cones, made from tuile *dough, or in salads. You could simply place a tiny scoop of sorbet on a spoon or in a pretty little cup for your guests.*

Like foams, sorbets should be handled sensibly when it comes to quantities. Some ice-cream makers sold for the home kitchen don't allow you to make small batches, although some professional machines and PacoJets do. Happily, sorbets keep for at least a month in the freezer, so you can indulge in these glorious flavors for weeks. The recipes here yield about three cups of sorbet.

Put scoops on top of salads or use them to create your own hot-and-cold dishes by spooning a little sorbet on top of grilled fish, chicken, foie gras, or anything else that piques your imagination.

PEA-MINT SORBET

makes about 3 cups

Cooks have paired peas and mint for generations, and I am no exception. I love the fresh, light flavors in this savory sorbet. Let it stand on its own or serve it in an almond cone.

7 cups frozen peas	1¾ cups plus 2 tablespoons
¼ cup fresh mint leaves	Simple Syrup (page 251)
	2 teaspoons salt

1. In a large pot of boiling water, blanch the peas and mint leaves until the peas turn bright green. (Frozen peas cook quickly and may be done even before the water returns to a boil. To test for doneness, bite into a pea.) Drain and immediately submerge in cold water. Drain again.

2. Transfer half the peas to a blender and puree. Pass the puree through a *chinois* or fine-mesh sieve into a large bowl. Puree the remaining peas and strain into the same bowl. Stir in as much water as needed for a fluid consistency. Strain through a *chinois* or fine-mesh sieve into a large pitcher. Mix in the syrup and salt.

3. If using a conventional ice-cream machine, cover and refrigerate the mixture for at least 2 hours or until thoroughly chilled. Freeze in the ice-cream machine according to the manufacturer's directions. Put the frozen sorbet in a chilled container, press plastic wrap against the surface, and cover. Freeze until ready to serve.

4. If using a PacoJet, pour the mixture into a PacoJet canister and freeze completely. Place the canister in the machine and spin, according to the manufacturer's directions.

5. To serve, scoop 1-tablespoon mounds of sorbet into almond *tuile* cones (see page 234) or small bowls.

makes about 3 cups

As soon as I thought of it, I loved the idea of serving a Champagne amuse. Champagne is a celebratory wine—why not experience it in an amuse at the beginning of a special meal? But plain Champagne was not enough. At Tru, my chef de cuisine, Mark Andelbredt, suggested adding saffron to the Champagne for a twist and it worked wonderfully. The result was this light, refreshing, and very elegant amuse. Serve it in an orange cone.

I love using saffron, which arguably used to be the most precious of all spices. As long ago as the Middle Ages, it was a status symbol in Europe, where it was often used to coat cooked food for a showy presentation. For centuries, Abruzzi, Italy, was one of the most famous saffron-producing regions, and Abruzzi saffron was long regarded as the best there was. Today, saffron is used less frequently in cooking, although some dishes, such as Spanish paella and risotto Milanese, rely on it. Saffron is the dried stigmas of crocuses, which bloom for only a few weeks. Because the stigmas are extracted by hand, it is very costly. For the best flavor, buy saffron from a reputable dealer.

One 750-milliliter bottle Champagne or sparkling wine	½ cup plus 2 tablespoons Simple Syrup (page 251)
1 tablespoon saffron threads	Fresh lemon juice
3½ tablespoons red verjus (see Note)	Salt

1. Stir the Champagne and saffron together in a medium-sized saucepan and bring to a boil over high heat. Reduce the heat and simmer for 15 to 20 minutes or until reduced by half. Remove from the heat, stir in the verjus, and set aside to cool.

2. When cool, whisk in the syrup. Add the lemon juice and salt to taste.

3. If using a conventional ice-cream machine, transfer the mixture to a pitcher, cover, and refrigerate for at least 2 hours or until thoroughly chilled. Freeze in the ice-cream machine according to the manufacturer's directions. Put the frozen sorbet in a chilled container, press plastic wrap against the surface, and cover. Freeze until ready to serve.

4. If using a PacoJet, pour the mixture into a PacoJet canister and freeze completely. Place the canister in the machine and spin, according to the manufacturer's directions.

5. To serve, scoop 1-tablespoon mounds of sorbet into orange *tuile* cones (see page 238) or small bowls.

NOTE: Verjus, or verjuice, is an acidic liquid made most commonly from unripened grapes. It is sour enough to be used much as lemon juice or vinegar. Look for it in specialty food markets. While not widely available, it is getting increasingly easy to find.

makes about 3 cups

You will need a lot of garlic cloves for this rich-tasting sorbet (as my friend Chef Emeril Lagasse always says, "There's never, never, never enough garlic!" And I agree: the more, the better), but after you peel them, most of the work is done. I blanch the cloves several times to tame their flavor so that the sorbet is mellow tasting, never overpowering. How often you blanch them depends on your taste and the strength of the garlic. You can serve this in Parmigiano-Reggiano cones.

70 cloves garlic, peeled	7 tablespoons Simple Syrup
(4 to 5 heads)	(page 251)
1 cup plus 1 tablespoon water	Salt

1. Put the garlic cloves in a large pot of boiling water. As soon as the water returns to a boil, remove from the heat. Drain and immediately submerge in cold water. Drain again. Repeat the blanching-and-shocking process 5 or 6 times.

2. Pass the garlic through a *chinois* or fine-mesh sieve into a bowl. Add the water and syrup and mix well. Season to taste with salt.

3. If using a conventional ice-cream machine, cover and refrigerate the mixture for at least 2 hours or until thoroughly chilled. Freeze in the ice-cream machine according to the manufacturer's directions. Put the frozen sorbet in a chilled container, press plastic wrap against the surface, and cover. Freeze until ready to serve.

4. If using a PacoJet, pour the mixture into a PacoJet canister and freeze completely. Place the canister in the machine and spin, according to the manufacturer's directions.

5. To serve, scoop 1-tablespoon mounds of sorbet into Parmigiano-Reggiano *tuile* cones (see page 235) or small bowls.

A SALAD OF
CUCUMBER SORBET

---

serves 6; makes about 3 cups sorbet

Summertime is when I most appreciate the fresh, crisp flavor of cucumbers, so after I tried cucumber juice, cucumber sorbet was the obvious next step. I sweeten it with a little simple syrup and brighten it with lemon for a surprisingly cool savory sorbet. I also love this served in a black pepper cone (see page 236) or on a tomato and red onion salad.

2 cups cucumber juice (see page 184)	6 to 8 ounces frisée, microgreens, or micro pea shoots
½ cup plus 1 tablespoon light corn syrup	Extra-virgin olive oil
¼ cup Simple Syrup (page 251)	Fresh lemon juice
1 tablespoon fresh lemon juice	Mint leaves, for garnishing
Salt	Salt and freshly ground black pepper

1. Strain the cucumber juice through a *chinois* or fine-mesh sieve into a pitcher. Add the corn syrup, simple syrup, and lemon juice and stir well. Season to taste with salt.

2. If using a conventional ice-cream machine, cover and refrigerate the mixture for at least 2 hours or until thoroughly chilled. Freeze in the ice-cream machine according to the manufacturer's directions. Put the frozen sorbet in a chilled container, press plastic wrap against the surface, and cover. Freeze until ready to serve.

3. If using a PacoJet, pour the mixture into a PacoJet canister and freeze completely. Place the canister in the machine and spin, according to the manufacturer's directions.

4. Toss the greens with a little olive oil, lemon juice, and salt and pepper to taste.

5. To serve, spoon the greens on a small plate. Scoop 1-tablespoon mounds of sorbet on top of the greens. Garnish each scoop with a mint leaf and a little cracked pepper.

makes about 3 cups

Letting this sorbet melt on your tongue is like eating sweet, full-flavored, ice-cold pumpkin pie. I developed this one year when I just couldn't let go of summer's guilty pleasures but still ached for the round, deep flavors of autumn. I make this either with canned pumpkin puree or fresh puree. Canned is easier to use than fresh pumpkin and just as tasty; buy the unsweetened kind. Try this in an orange cone at your next Thanksgiving dinner.

One 15-ounce can unsweetened pumpkin puree, or one 2- to 3-pound cooking pumpkin, roasted (see Note)	1¼ cups Simple Syrup (page 251)
	½ cup light corn syrup
	½ teaspoon ground cinnamon
3 cups water	Salt and freshly ground black pepper

1. Put half of the pumpkin puree, 1½ cups of the water, half of the simple syrup, and ¼ cup of the corn syrup in a blender and puree. Strain through a *chinois* or fine-mesh sieve into a large pitcher. Put the remaining pumpkin puree, 1½ cups water, simple syrup, and ¼ cup corn syrup in the blender and puree. Strain through a *chinois* or fine-mesh sieve into the same pitcher. Mix in the cinnamon and season to taste with salt and pepper.

2. If using a conventional ice-cream machine, cover and refrigerate the mixture for at least 2 hours or until thoroughly chilled. Freeze in the ice-cream machine according to the manufacturer's directions. Put the frozen sorbet in a chilled container, press plastic wrap against the surface, and cover. Freeze until ready to serve.

3. If using a PacoJet, pour the mixture into a PacoJet canister and freeze completely. Place the canister in the machine and spin, according to the manufacturer's directions.

4. To serve, scoop 1-tablespoon mounds of sorbet into orange *tuile* cones (see page 238) or small bowls.

NOTE: To roast a pumpkin and make puree, cut the pumpkin into large pieces, scrape off the seeds, rub the pumpkin flesh with olive oil, and season with salt and pepper. Lay the pieces in a shallow roasting pan, skin side up, cover tightly with foil, and roast for 45 to 60 minutes at 325°F or until the flesh is soft. Scrape the flesh from the pumpkin skin and mash into a puree. A 5- to 6-pound pumpkin yields about 4 cups of puree, so you might have some left over. It freezes well.

CARROT-CLEMENTINE SORBET

makes about 3 cups

I can't imagine making this sorbet during any other season but winter, when clementines are plentiful in the markets. Although there is no cream in the recipe, the sorbet reminds me of Creamsicle bars—the smooth, pale-orange-covered vanilla ice cream we all loved as children. I constantly reach for clementines and other citrus fruits to elevate the flavor of foods, using citrus juice the way other chefs use salt and pepper. Serve this in an orange or a black pepper cone.

1½ cups carrot juice (see page 184)	¾ cup Simple Syrup (page 251)
½ cup clementine juice (see page 184)	3 tablespoons light corn syrup
	Salt

1. Strain the carrot and clementine juices separately or together through a *chinois* or fine-mesh sieve into a pitcher. Add the simple syrup and corn syrup and stir until combined. Season to taste with salt.

2. If using a conventional ice-cream machine, cover and refrigerate the mixture for at least 2 hours or until thoroughly chilled. Freeze in the ice-cream machine according to the manufacturer's directions. Put the frozen sorbet in a chilled container, press plastic wrap against the surface, and cover. Freeze until ready to serve.

3. If using a PacoJet, pour the mixture into a PacoJet canister and freeze completely. Place the canister in the machine and spin, according to the manufacturer's directions.

4. To serve, scoop 1-tablespoon mounds of sorbet into orange or black pepper *tuile* cones (see page 238 or 236) or small bowls.

CABERNET-SHALLOT SORBET

WITH PISTACHIO WAVES

serves 6; makes about 3 cups sorbet

When you freeze a good Cabernet Sauvignon with simple syrup, you end up with a rich, winy sorbet and a lovely amuse. *But don't stop there. Serve this later in the meal with a cheese or fruit course, or, if you make it in the summer, take it on a picnic as a refreshing dessert.*

1 teaspoon olive oil	½ cup Simple Syrup (page 251)
1 shallot, finely diced	½ cup glucose, a scant 5 ounces, or
One 750-milliliter bottle Cabernet	light corn syrup (see Note)
Sauvignon	6 Pistachio Waves (recipe follows)

1. Heat the oil in a small sauté pan over medium-low heat. Add the shallot and cook, stirring frequently, for about 5 minutes or until the shallot is nicely browned. Add ½ cup of the wine and bring to a boil, stirring the bottom of the pan with a wooden spoon to deglaze. Remove from the heat.

2. Put the remaining wine in a large saucepan along with the shallot-wine mixture and bring to a boil over high heat. Reduce the heat and simmer for 40 to 50 minutes or until the wine is reduced by half, or to about 1½ cups. Remove from the heat and stir in the simple syrup and glucose or corn syrup. Allow to cool to room temperature. Strain through a *chinois* or fine-mesh sieve into a large bowl, reserving the shallot.

3. Return the shallot to the wine and pour the mixture into a pitcher or bowl.

4. If using a conventional ice-cream machine, cover and refrigerate the mixture for at least 2 hours or until thoroughly chilled. Freeze in the ice-cream machine according to the manufacturer's directions. Put the frozen sorbet in a chilled container, press plastic wrap against the surface, and cover. Freeze until ready to serve.

5. If using a PacoJet, pour the mixture into a PacoJet canister and freeze completely. Place the canister in the machine and spin, according to the manufacturer's directions.

6. To serve, place 1 pistachio wave on a small plate, seasoned side up, and scoop a tiny mound of sorbet into the central indentation. Repeat to make 5 more servings.

NOTE: Glucose is sold in pharmacies and many supermarkets and specialty stores.

PISTACHIO WAVES

makes 6 waves

These were first made by the brilliant and amazing pastry team at Tru.

1 sheet *pâte à bric* (see Note)	1 tablespoon finely chopped
Clarified butter (see Note)	pistachio nuts
	Salt and freshly ground black pepper

1. Preheat the oven to 350°F. Line a baking sheet with parchment paper.

2. Spread out the sheet of pastry on a work surface and generously brush with butter. Using a pastry or pizza wheel, cut the sheet into six 1-by-6-inch strips. Sprinkle with the pistachio nuts and season to taste with salt and pepper.

3. Place 3 cannoli molds side by side on the prepared baking sheet. One at a time, weave 3 of the pastry strips over and under the molds, giving each strip a shape that resembles 2 hills with a valley in between. Weight the overhanging ends of the pastry with small, heavy objects (extra cannoli molds, for example). Keep the remaining pastry strips covered with plastic wrap to prevent them from drying out.

4. Bake the waves for 5 to 7 minutes or until golden brown.

5. When cool enough to handle, remove the molds and carefully transfer the pistachio waves to a wire rack to cool completely.

6. Repeat to form and bake 3 more waves.

NOTE: *Pâte à bric* is also known as *pâte feuilletée* or *feuilletage*. It's very thin pastry made with flour, salt, water, and oil. It contains no butter. Substitute phyllo pastry for it if you can't find it in specialty food markets.

To clarify butter, melt at least 1 cup of unsalted butter over low heat in a small pan. Let the butter simmer for 8 to 10 minutes, during which time water will evaporate and the milk solids will collect on the bottom of the pan. Skim any foam that gathers on the top of the butter. Very carefully, pour the clear liquid butter through a *chinois* or fine-mesh sieve into a glass measuring cup or jar. Take care that the white milk solids remain in the pan. Discard the milk solids. Allow the golden-colored butter to cool completely before covering and refrigerating. Clarified butter keeps very well for up to 2 months.

SALSIFY SORBET

m a k e s   a b o u t   2 ½   c u p s

Because I love the sensation of hot and cold food together, I was intrigued by the idea of serving a scoop of ice-cold salsify sorbet alongside hot sautéed foie gras. As the sorbet melted, it blended wickedly with the fat of the foie gras. I loved this indulgence but also thought a scoop of salsify sorbet on its own would taste great as an amuse. *Serve this in a black pepper or an almond cone.*

We don't eat much salsify in the United States; it's far more popular in Europe, where it's eaten mainly in Spain, Italy, and Greece. This sorbet is a good way to try the long white-fleshed root vegetable, sometimes called oyster plant because of its flavor. Look for firm salsify—it can be as long as a foot and is usually about two inches in diameter. Some rarer varieties of salsify are golden, while others are practically black; all taste similar.

1¾ pounds salsify	10 black peppercorns
3 cups milk	1 bay leaf
1½ cups sugar	

1. Trim, peel, and cut the salsify into 1½- to 2-inch segments. Drop the segments into a large bowl of acidulated water as soon as they are cut to prevent discoloration.

2. Drain the salsify and transfer to a large saucepan with the milk, sugar, peppercorns, and bay leaf. Bring to a boil over medium-high heat. Reduce the heat and simmer for 15 to 20 minutes or until the salsify is tender. Set aside to cool.

3. Remove the bay leaf. Transfer the contents of the saucepan to a blender and puree. You may have to do this in batches. Strain through a *chinois* or fine-mesh sieve into a large pitcher.

4. If using a conventional ice-cream machine, cover and refrigerate the mixture for at least 2 hours or until thoroughly chilled. Freeze in the ice-cream machine according to the manufacturer's directions. Put the frozen sorbet in a chilled container, press plastic wrap against the surface, and cover. Freeze until ready to serve.

5. If using a PacoJet, pour the mixture into a PacoJet canister and freeze completely. Place the canister in the machine and spin, according to the manufacturer's directions.

6. To serve, scoop 1-tablespoon mounds of sorbet into black pepper or almond *tuile* cones (see page 236 or 234) or small bowls.

TUILES

As soon as these triangular tuiles *are baked, it's important to work quickly to wrap them around the cone mold while they are soft and pliable. The* tuile *recipes make far more cones than you will need, but not only is working with a smaller quantity of batter difficult, but the final product will not be as successful. Use the leftover batter to make crispy cookies.*

ALMOND TUILES

makes about 30 cones

³/₄ cup plus 3 tablespoons all-purpose flour	10 tablespoons (1¹/₄ sticks) unsalted butter, softened
¹/₄ teaspoon salt	¹/₄ cup sugar
¹/₄ teaspoon freshly ground white pepper	1¹/₂ tablespoons honey
	4 large egg whites
¹/₄ cup almond flour	Ground toasted almonds

1. Preheat the oven to 350°F. Line a half sheet pan with a silicone baking mat or grease and flour the pan and then line the pan with parchment paper. Have ready a 4-inch triangle mold and at least 1 metal or wooden cone mold.

2. Whisk the all-purpose flour, salt, white pepper, and almond flour together in a small bowl. Set aside.

3. In the bowl of an electric mixer fitted with the paddle attachment, beat the butter at medium speed until creamy. Add the sugar and honey and beat until the mixture is pale in color. Reduce the speed to low and add the dry ingredients, beating until combined. With the mixer on high speed, add the egg whites one at a time and beat until mixed. Beat the batter until very smooth.

4. Place the triangle mold on the prepared pan and spread a thin layer of batter in it. Remove the mold and repeat to make 5 more *tuiles*. Sprinkle toasted ground almonds over the batter.

5. Bake in the middle of the oven for 3 minutes or until set and light golden. Using a small off-

set spatula, remove each *tuile* from the baking sheet and carefully roll around the cone mold. Gently remove the mold and then set the cone on a wire rack to crisp up and cool completely.

6. Make additional cones with the remaining batter.

PARMIGIANO-REGGIANO TUILES

makes about 30 cones

1 cup all-purpose flour	10 tablespoons (1¼ sticks) unsalted
¼ teaspoon salt	butter, softened
¼ teaspoon freshly ground white	6 tablespoons sugar
pepper	4 large egg whites
2 ounces Parmigiano-Reggiano	
cheese, finely grated	

1. Preheat the oven to 350°F. Line a half sheet pan with a silicone baking mat or grease and flour the pan and then line the pan with parchment paper. Have ready a 4-inch triangle mold and at least 1 metal or wooden cone mold.

2. Whisk the flour, salt, and white pepper together in a small bowl. Pass the grated cheese through a *chinois* or fine-mesh sieve and stir into the flour. Set aside.

3. In the bowl of an electric mixer fitted with the paddle attachment, beat the butter at medium speed until creamy. Add the sugar and beat until the mixture is pale in color. Reduce the speed to low and add the dry ingredients, beating until combined. With the mixer on high speed, add the egg whites one at a time and beat until mixed. Beat the batter until very smooth.

4. Place the triangle mold on the prepared pan and spread a thin layer of batter in it. Remove the mold and repeat to make 5 more *tuiles*.

5. Bake in the middle of the oven for 3 minutes or until set and light golden. Using a small offset spatula, remove each *tuile* from the baking sheet and carefully roll around the cone mold. Gently remove the mold and then set the cone on a wire rack to crisp up and cool completely.

6. Make additional cones with the remaining batter.

BLACK PEPPER TUILES

makes about 30 cones

1 cup all-purpose flour	10 tablespoons (1 1/4 sticks) unsalted
1/4 teaspoon salt	butter, softened
1/4 teaspoon freshly ground black	1/4 cup sugar
pepper, plus more as needed	1 tablespoon honey
	4 large egg whites

1. Preheat the oven to 350°F. Line a half sheet pan with a silicone baking mat or grease and flour the pan and then line the pan with parchment paper. Have ready a 4-inch triangle mold and at least 1 metal or wooden cone mold.

2. Whisk the flour, salt, and 1/4 teaspoon pepper together in a small bowl. Set aside.

3. In the bowl of an electric mixer fitted with the paddle attachment, beat the butter at medium speed until creamy. Add the sugar and honey and beat until the mixture is pale in color. Reduce the speed to low and add the dry ingredients, beating until combined. With the mixer on high speed, add the egg whites one at a time and beat until mixed. Beat the batter until very smooth.

4. Place the triangle mold on the prepared pan and spread a thin layer of batter in it. Remove the mold and repeat to make 5 more *tuiles*. Sprinkle additional pepper over the *tuiles*.

5. Bake in the middle of the oven for 3 minutes or until set and light golden. Using a small offset spatula, remove each *tuile* from the baking sheet and carefully roll around the cone mold. Gently remove the mold and then set the cone on a wire rack to crisp up and cool completely.

6. Make additional cones with the remaining batter.

makes about 30 cones

1 cup plus 1 tablespoon all-purpose flour	¼ cup sugar
¼ teaspoon salt	1 tablespoon honey
¼ teaspoon freshly ground white pepper	2 teaspoons sesame oil
10 tablespoons (1¼ sticks) unsalted butter, softened	4 large egg whites
	Toasted black and white sesame seeds

1. Preheat the oven to 350°F. Line a half sheet pan with a silicone baking mat or grease and flour the pan and then line the pan with parchment paper. Have ready a 4-inch triangle mold and at least 1 metal or wooden cone mold.

2. Whisk the flour, salt, and white pepper together in a small bowl. Set aside.

3. In the bowl of an electric mixer fitted with the paddle attachment, beat the butter at medium speed until creamy. Add the sugar, honey, and sesame oil and beat until the mixture is pale in color. Reduce the speed to low and add the dry ingredients, beating until combined. With the mixer on high speed, add the egg whites one at a time and beat until mixed. Beat the batter until very smooth.

4. Place the triangle mold on the prepared pan and spread a thin layer of batter in it. Remove the mold and repeat to make 5 more *tuiles*. Sprinkle black and white sesame seeds over the batter.

5. Bake in the middle of the oven for 3 minutes or until set and light golden. Using a small offset spatula, remove each *tuile* from the baking sheet and carefully roll around the cone mold. Gently remove the mold and then set the cone on a wire rack to crisp up and cool completely.

6. Make additional cones with the remaining batter.

makes about 30 cones

1 cup all-purpose flour	¼ cup sugar
¼ teaspoon salt	1½ tablespoons honey
¼ teaspoon freshly ground white pepper	1 tablespoon grated orange zest
	½ teaspoon orange extract
10 tablespoons (1¼ sticks) unsalted butter, softened	4 large egg whites

1. Preheat the oven to 350°F. Line a half sheet pan with a silicone baking mat or grease and flour the pan and then line the pan with parchment paper. Have ready a 4-inch triangle mold and at least 1 metal or wooden cone mold.

2. Whisk the flour, salt, and white pepper together in a small bowl. Set aside.

3. In the bowl of an electric mixer fitted with the paddle attachment, beat the butter at medium speed until creamy. Add the sugar, honey, orange zest, and orange extract and beat until the mixture is pale in color. Reduce the speed to low and add the dry ingredients, beating until combined. With the mixer on high speed, add the egg whites one at a time and beat until mixed. Beat the batter until very smooth.

4. Place the triangle mold on the prepared pan and spread a thin layer of batter in it. Remove the mold and repeat to make 5 more *tuiles*.

5. Bake in the middle of the oven for 3 minutes or until set and light golden. Using a small offset spatula, remove each *tuile* from the baking sheet and carefully roll around the cone mold. Gently remove the mold and then set the cone on a wire rack to crisp up and cool completely.

6. Make additional cones with the remaining batter.

CHAPTER TEN

basic recipes

makes about 8 cups

1 pound meaty beef bones	1 tablespoon fresh thyme leaves
2 tablespoons vegetable oil	1 tablespoon black peppercorns
1 cup chopped onions	2 bay leaves
½ cup chopped carrots	½ cup dry red or dry white wine
½ cup chopped celery	(optional)
2 tablespoons tomato paste	10 cups water

1. Rinse the beef bones well under cold water to remove any blood. Set aside.

2. Heat the oil in a large saucepan over low heat. Add the onions, carrots, and celery to the pan and cook, stirring occasionally, for about 5 minutes or until the vegetables are softened but not colored. Stir in the tomato paste, thyme, peppercorns, and bay leaves.

3. If using the wine, add it now and stir to incorporate the tomato paste. Add the bones and water. Bring to a boil over medium heat. Carefully skim off any fat and froth that float to the surface of the liquid. Reduce the heat to low and simmer gently for 2 to 3 hours or until somewhat reduced and flavorful.

4. Strain the stock through a *chinois* or fine-mesh sieve into a large bowl. Discard the bones and vegetables. Allow to cool in an ice bath. Cover and refrigerate until chilled, and then remove the layer of congealed fat from the surface.

5. Transfer to covered storage containers and refrigerate for up to 3 days or freeze for up to 3 months.

CHICKEN STOCK

makes about 8 cups

1 pound chicken bones	1 tablespoon fresh thyme leaves
2 tablespoons vegetable oil	1 tablespoon black peppercorns
1 cup chopped onions	2 bay leaves
½ cup chopped carrots	½ cup dry white wine (optional)
½ cup chopped celery	10 cups water

1. Rinse the chicken bones well under cold water to remove any blood. Set aside.
2. Heat the oil in a large saucepan over low heat. Add the onions, carrots, and celery to the pan and cook, stirring occasionally, for about 5 minutes or until the vegetables are softened but not colored. Stir in the thyme, peppercorns, and bay leaves.
3. If using the wine, add it now. Add the bones and water. Bring to a boil over medium heat. Carefully skim off any fat and froth that float to the surface of the liquid. Reduce the heat to low and simmer gently for 2 to 3 hours or until somewhat reduced and flavorful.
4. Strain the stock through a *chinois* or fine-mesh sieve into a large bowl. Discard the bones and vegetables. Allow to cool in an ice bath. Cover and refrigerate until chilled, and then remove the layer of congealed fat from the surface.
5. Transfer to covered storage containers and refrigerate for up to 3 days or freeze for up to 3 months.

makes about 8 cups

1 pound duck bones	1 tablespoon fresh thyme leaves
2 tablespoons vegetable oil	1 tablespoon black peppercorns
1 cup chopped onions	2 bay leaves
½ cup chopped carrots	½ cup dry white wine (optional)
½ cup chopped celery	10 cups water
2 tablespoons tomato paste	

1. Rinse the duck bones well under cold water to remove any blood. Set aside.

2. Heat the oil in a large saucepan over low heat. Add the onions, carrots, and celery to the pan and cook, stirring occasionally, for about 5 minutes or until the vegetables are softened but not colored. Stir in the tomato paste, thyme, peppercorns, and bay leaves.

3. If using the wine, add it now and stir to incorporate the tomato paste. Add the bones and water. Bring to a boil over medium heat. Carefully skim off any fat and froth that float to the surface of the liquid. Reduce the heat to low and simmer gently for 2 to 3 hours or until somewhat reduced and flavorful.

4. Strain the stock through a *chinois* or fine-mesh sieve into a large bowl. Discard the bones and vegetables. Allow to cool in an ice bath. Cover and refrigerate until chilled, and then remove the layer of congealed fat from the surface.

5. Transfer to covered storage containers and refrigerate for up to 3 days or freeze for up to 3 months.

VEGETABLE STOCK

makes about 10 cups

3 tablespoons vegetable oil	1 tablespoon chopped fresh thyme
2 cups chopped onions	1 tablespoon black peppercorns
1 cup chopped carrots	2 bay leaves
1 cup chopped celery	½ cup dry white wine (optional)
½ cup chopped button mushrooms	10 cups water
2 cloves garlic, chopped	

1. Heat the oil in a large saucepan over low heat. Add the onions, carrots, celery, mushrooms, and garlic to the pan. Cook, stirring occasionally, for about 5 minutes or until the vegetables are softened but not colored. Stir in the thyme, peppercorns, and bay leaves.

2. If using the wine, add it now along with the water. Bring to a boil over medium heat. Carefully skim off any fat and froth that float to the surface of the liquid. Reduce the heat to low and gently simmer the stock for 30 minutes.

3. Strain the stock through a *chinois* or fine-mesh sieve into a large bowl. Discard the vegetables. Allow to cool in an ice bath. Cover and refrigerate until chilled, and then remove the layer of congealed fat from the surface.

4. Transfer to covered storage containers and refrigerate for up to 3 days or freeze for up to 3 months.

CITRUS VINAIGRETTE

makes about 1 cup

1 lemon	½ cup olive oil
1 lime	Salt and freshly ground black pepper
1 orange	

1. Squeeze the juices from the lemon, lime, and orange into the container of a blender.
2. With the motor running, slowly add the oil and blend until emulsified.
3. Strain the vinaigrette through a *chinois* or fine-mesh sieve into a small glass or ceramic bowl and season to taste with salt and pepper. Use immediately or refrigerate the vinaigrette in a tightly lidded nonreactive container for up to 2 weeks. Whisk well before using.

TRUFFLE VINAIGRETTE

makes about 3/4 cup

3 fresh black truffles (see Note)	1 tablespoon Dijon mustard
½ cup plus 2 tablespoons truffle juice (see Note)	Juice of ½ lemon
	½ cup white truffle oil
2 tablespoons sherry vinegar	Salt and freshly ground black pepper

1. In a blender, combine the truffles, truffle juice, vinegar, mustard, and lemon juice. Puree until smooth.
2. With the motor running, slowly add the oil and blend until emulsified.
3. Transfer to a small glass or ceramic bowl and season to taste with salt and pepper. Use immediately or refrigerate the vinaigrette in a tightly lidded nonreactive container for up to 2 weeks. Whisk well before using.

NOTE: You can buy truffle juice in specialty stores. I use white truffle oil, but you may use black truffle oil if you prefer it. The same goes for fresh truffles: I suggest black truffles, but if white truffles are in season and you can find them, use them.

BACON VINAIGRETTE

makes about ¹/₂ cup

4 ounces thick-cut bacon, cut into ¹/₄-inch cubes	1 teaspoon Dijon mustard
2 tablespoons sherry vinegar	Salt and freshly ground black pepper

1. In a small skillet or sauté pan, cook the bacon over medium heat for 8 to 10 minutes or until the fat is rendered and the bacon is crispy.
2. Remove from the heat and allow the bacon and bacon fat to cool slightly. Stir in the vinegar and mustard. Season to taste with salt and pepper and serve warm.

ALMOND VINAIGRETTE

makes about 1¹/₂ cups

¹/₄ cup almond oil	2 tablespoons Champagne vinegar
¹/₄ cup olive oil	Salt and freshly ground black pepper
³/₄ cup toasted sliced almonds	

1. Combine the two oils in a glass measuring cup with a spout.
2. Put the almonds and vinegar in a blender and puree until smooth and pastelike. With the motor running, slowly add the oils and blend until emulsified.
3. Transfer to a small glass or ceramic bowl and season to taste with salt and pepper. Use immediately or refrigerate the vinaigrette in a tightly lidded nonreactive container for up to 3 days. Whisk well before using.

PESTO OIL

makes about 1 cup

2 cups fresh basil leaves	Juice from ½ orange
1 teaspoon toasted pine nuts	1 cup grapeseed oil
½ teaspoon minced garlic	Salt

1. In a saucepan filled with boiling water, blanch the basil leaves for about 10 seconds or until they turn bright green. Drain and immediately submerge in cold water. Drain again.
2. Put the drained basil leaves and the pine nuts, garlic, and orange juice in a blender. With the motor running, slowly add the grapeseed oil and blend until pureed.
3. Strain the infused oil through a *chinois* or fine-mesh sieve into a small glass or ceramic bowl. Season to taste with salt. Use immediately or refrigerate the pesto oil in a tightly lidded nonreactive container for up to 4 days.

BUTTERMILK CRACKERS

makes enough for 6 to 10 servings

1¼ cups all-purpose flour, plus more as needed	5 tablespoons unsalted butter, cut into ½-inch cubes
1½ teaspoons sugar	½ cup plus 2 tablespoons buttermilk
Pinch of salt, plus more as needed	1 large egg white, lightly beaten
	Freshly ground black pepper

1. Preheat the oven to 350°F and position a rack in the center of the oven. Line a jelly-roll pan or a large baking sheet with parchment paper.

2. In the bowl of an electric mixer fitted with the paddle attachment, combine 1¼ cups flour, sugar, and salt and mix at low speed until combined. Add the butter and mix until the mixture resembles coarse crumbs. Add the buttermilk and continue to mix until the liquid is absorbed and the dough starts to come together. Do not overmix.

3. Turn the dough out onto a lightly floured work surface. Shape into a disk. Wrap in plastic wrap and refrigerate for at least 1 hour or until firm enough to roll out.

4. Lightly dust the work surface and a rolling pin with flour. Roll out the dough into a very thin sheet, about ¼ inch thick, dusting the work surface and dough with additional flour as needed. Prick the sheet of dough all over with a fork. Transfer the dough to the prepared pan. Unless the work surface is dusted with flour, the dough might stick. Use a spatula or another tool to release it gently from the surface. Brush the dough with some of the egg white and sprinkle with salt and pepper.

5. Bake in the middle of the oven for 6 to 10 minutes or until golden brown. Transfer to a wire rack to cool completely. Break into irregularly shaped pieces to serve.

BRIOCHE

makes one 9-by-5-inch loaf

One ¼-ounce package active dry yeast	¼ cup sugar
2 tablespoons warm water	1 teaspoon salt
1½ cups all-purpose flour	4 large eggs
1¼ cups plus 2 tablespoons bread flour	½ pound (2 sticks) unsalted butter, cut into small pieces

1. Sprinkle the yeast over the water. Set aside for about 5 minutes.
2. Put the flours, sugar, and salt in the bowl of an electric mixer fitted with the dough hook. Beat for 1 minute or until mixed.
3. Add the eggs and the yeast mixture. With the mixer on medium speed, beat until smooth.
4. Add the butter and mix until all the butter is incorporated.
5. Cover the bowl with plastic wrap and refrigerate for 24 hours. It will be risen.
6. Without punching it down, remove the dough from the bowl and roll into a log. Transfer the dough to a 9-by-5-inch loaf pan and cover with plastic wrap. Set aside in a warm, draft-free place for 2 to 3 hours or until it rises so that it touches the plastic wrap.
7. Preheat the oven to 350°F.
8. Bake for 45 to 60 minutes or until the crust is lightly browned and the bread is cooked through in the center.
9. Remove from the pan immediately and allow to cool completely on a wire rack.

TARTLET DOUGH

makes 6 to 8 tartlet shells

½ cup plus 1 tablespoon crème fraîche, homemade (page 252) or store-bought 1 large egg yolk	2¼ cups all-purpose flour, plus more as needed ½ teaspoon salt 9 tablespoons unsalted butter, cut into ½-inch cubes

1. Preheat the oven to 325°F and position a rack in the center of the oven. Have ready six to eight 1-inch-diameter tartlet pans and a baking sheet.

2. In a small bowl, whisk the crème fraîche and egg yolk until blended. Set aside.

3. Put the flour and salt in the bowl of an electric mixer fitted with the paddle attachment and mix at low speed until combined. Add the butter and mix until the mixture is the consistency of sand. Add the crème fraîche mixture and continue to mix until the liquid is absorbed and the dough is starting to come together. Do not overmix.

4. Turn the dough out onto a lightly floured work surface. Shape into a disk. Wrap in plastic wrap and refrigerate for at least 1 hour or until firm enough to roll out.

5. Lightly dust the work surface and a rolling pin with flour. Roll out the dough into a very thin sheet, about ¼ inch thick, dusting the work surface and dough with additional flour as needed. Cut out rounds of dough with a biscuit cutter slightly larger than the diameter of the tartlet pans. Center each round in the bottom of a tartlet pan and press the dough onto the bottom and up the sides of the pan without stretching. Place the tartlet shells on a baking sheet and refrigerate for at least 1 hour before baking.

6. Bake in the middle of the oven for 8 to 10 minutes or until light brown. Transfer the baking sheet with the shells to a wire rack to cool completely.

CUCUMBER ASPIC

makes 1 thin layer in a 9-by-12-inch jelly-roll pan

2 cups cucumber juice (page 184)	9 sheets gelatin
	Salt

1. Put the cucumber juice in a medium-sized saucepan over low heat just until warm. As soon as the juice is warm, remove from the heat. Do not let it simmer.

2. Meanwhile, fill a large bowl with cold water. Gently drop the gelatin sheets into the water, several at a time, until all are submerged. Let soften and bloom for about 5 minutes.

3. Using your hands, lift the gelatin sheets from the water and squeeze them gently between your fingers. Transfer to the cucumber juice. Stir gently until dissolved. Season to taste with salt.

4. Pour the juice into a small jelly-roll pan, or other rimmed metal pan measuring about 9 by 12 inches, and allow to cool at room temperature. Refrigerate, uncovered, for about 2 hours or until needed. When the jelly is set, cover with plastic wrap and keep refrigerated until needed.

VEGETABLE ASPIC

makes about 2 cups

2 cups Vegetable Stock (page 243)	Salt
20 sheets gelatin	

1. Put the vegetable stock in a medium-sized saucepan and bring to a boil. As soon as the stock comes to a boil, remove from the heat.

2. Meanwhile, fill a large bowl with cold water. Gently drop the gelatin sheets into the water, several at a time, until all are submerged. Let soften and bloom for about 5 minutes.

3. Using your hands, lift the gelatin sheets from the water and squeeze them gently between your fingers. Transfer to the hot vegetable stock. Stir gently until dissolved. Season to taste with salt. Allow to cool to room temperature.

4. Transfer to a covered container and refrigerate until needed.

PICKLING SPICE BLEND

makes about 1 1/2 cups

1/4 cup fennel seeds	1/4 cup mustard seeds
2 tablespoons broken bay leaves	1 tablespoon red pepper flakes
1/4 cup whole allspice	2 tablespoons ground cinnamon
1/4 cup black peppercorns	

Put all the ingredients in a medium-sized bowl and toss until well mixed. Transfer to a tightly covered container.

SIMPLE SYRUP

makes about 1 cup

1/2 cup sugar	1 cup water

1. In a small saucepan set over medium heat, combine the sugar and water and stir until the sugar is dissolved. Raise the heat and bring to a boil. As soon as the mixture comes to a boil, remove from the heat and allow to cool.
2. Transfer to a covered container and refrigerate for up to 1 month or until needed.

CRÈME FRAÎCHE

makes about 2 cups

2 cups heavy cream	2 tablespoons buttermilk

1. Mix the cream and buttermilk together in a glass, ceramic, or other nonreactive bowl. Stir well, cover, and leave at room temperature for 10 to 12 hours or until clotted and the consistency of thick sour cream.
2. Refrigerate until needed. The crème fraîche will keep for about 1 week.

sources for hard-to-find
ingredients and equipment

Following are sources I use at the restaurant for much of our food and equipment. If there is something you cannot find from local purveyors, one of these merchants may well be able to help you. I want to thank these incredible vendors who help me so much and make what I do at Tru possible.

SEAFOOD AND FISH

Browne Trading
260 Commercial Street,
 Stop 3
Portland, ME 04101
Phone: (207) 766-2402
Fax: (207) 766-2404

Caviar Russe
46 Washington Street
Brooklyn, NY 11201
Phone: (718) 797-9090
Fax: (718) 643-2640

Collins Caviar
925 West Jackson Boulevard
Chicago, IL 60607
Phone: (312) 226-0342
Fax: (312) 226-2114

Fortune Fish
2442 North Seventy-seventh Street
Elmwood Park, IL 60707
Phone: (630) 860-7100

Honolulu Fish
1907 Democrat Street
Honolulu, HI 96819
Phone: (808) 833-1123
Fax: (888) 475-6244

International Marine
1021 South Railroad Avenue
San Mateo, CA 94402
Phone: (650) 341-0390
Fax: (650) 341-9798

M. F. Foley Fish Company
24 West Howell Street
Dorchester, MA 02125
Phone: (800) 225-9995
Fax: (617) 288-1300

Pierless Fish
Brooklyn Navy Yard
Brooklyn, NY 11205
Phone: (718) 222-4441

Plitt Seafood
1445 West Willow Street
Chicago, IL 60061
Phone: (773) 276-2200
Fax: (773) 276-3350

Seafood Merchants
900 Forest Edge Drive
Vernon Hills, IL 60061
Phone: (847) 634-0900
Fax: (847) 634-1351

Steve Connolly Seafood Company
34 Newmarket Square
Boston, MA 02118
Phone: (800) 225-5595

MEAT AND POULTRY

Jamison Farms (lamb)
171 Jamison Lane
Latrobe, PA 15650
Phone: (800) 237-5262

Joseph Baumgardner Meats
Phone: (312) 829-7762
Fax: (312) 829-8791

Millbrook Farms
Phone: (800) 774-3337
Fax: (845) 677-8457

Niman Ranch
940 Judson Avenue
Evanston, IL 60202
Phone: (847) 570-0200

Stockyards
340 North Oakley Boulevard
Chicago, IL 60612
Phone: (312) 733-6050
Fax: (312) 733-0738

Swan Creek Farms
10531 Wood Road
North Adam, MI 49262
Phone: (517) 523-3308

Wild Game
2475 North Elston Avenue
Chicago, IL 60647
Phone: (773) 227-0600
Fax: (773) 227-6775

PRODUCE

Chef's Garden
9009 Huron-Avery Road
Huron, OH 44839
Phone: (800) 289-4644

Earthly Delights
720 East Eldorado Street
Decatur, IL 62523
Phone: (800) 367-4709

Fresh and Wild
2917 Northeast Sixty-fifth Street
Vancouver, WA 98663
Phone: (360) 737-3652

George Cornille and Sons
60 West South Water Market Street
Chicago, IL 60608
Phone: (312) 226-1015
Fax: (312) 226-3016

Mid-West Foods
3100 West Thirty-sixth Street
Chicago, IL 60632
Phone: (773) 927-8870;
    (800) 930-4270
Fax: (773) 932-4280

Pacific Farms
88420 Highway 101
Florence, OR 97430
Phone: (541) 340-0000;
    (800) 927-2248
Fax: (541) 345-8050

Sid Wainer and Son
2301 Purchase Street
New Bedford, MA 20746
Phone: (800) 423-8333
Fax: (508) 999-6795

SPECIALTY PRODUCTS
AND SPICES

Anson Mills
1922-C Gervais Street
Columbus, SC 29201
Phone: (803) 467-4122
Fax: (803) 256-2463

European Imports
2475 North Elston Avenue
Chicago, IL 60647
Phone: (773) 227-0600
Fax: (773) 227-6775

Gourmand
728 South Dearborn Street
Chicago, IL 60605
Phone: (800) 627-7272
Fax: (703) 708-9393

Natural Juice
550 Clayton Court
Wood Dale, IL 60191
Phone: (630) 350-1700

Spiceland
6604 West Irving Park Road
Chicago, IL 60634
Phone: (773) 736-1000
Fax: (773) 736-1271

Tekla (cheese)
1456 North Dayton Street
Chicago, IL 60622
Phone: (312) 915-5914
Fax: (312) 943-0691

Urbani Truffle
2924 Fortieth Avenue
Long Island City, NY 11101
Phone: (718) 392-5050
Fax: (718) 392-1704

PASTRY SUPPLIES

Albert Uster
Phone: (800) 231-8154
Fax: (773) 761-5412

Nieman Brothers
3322 West Newport Avenue
Chicago, IL 60618
Phone: (773) 463-3000

EQUIPMENT

Boelter (kitchen supplies)
Phone: (847) 675-2963
Fax: (847) 675-0505

Chef's Catalog
(800) 884-2433

Tramonto Cuisine, Inc.
   (caviar staircases)
cheftramonto@aol.com
Phone: (847) 846-9697

PacoJet (for sorbet)
Phone: (212) 421-1106
Fax: (212) 421-1137

Pease Acrylics (molded plastics
   and acrylics)
1475 Busch Parkway
Buffalo Grove, IL 60089
Phone: (847) 419-1300
Fax: (847) 419-1381

Utsuwa-No-Yakata (china, glass,
   and bento boxes)
100 East Algonquin Road
Arlington Heights, IL 60005
Phone: (847) 640-0820

Williams-Sonoma
(877) 812-6235

index

Page numbers in *italic* refer to photographs.

Crackers, Buttermilk, 247

Heirloom Tomatoes "Panzanella Style," 32, *33*

cream:

Crème Fraîche, 252

Mascarpone Foam, 143

Smoked Salmon Parfait with Chive Oil, 87–89, *88*

Cream Cheese, Smoked Salmon Crepes with, 115–17, *116*

Crème Brûlée, Carrot, with Blood Orange Reduction and Carrot Sprouts, 50–51

Crème Fraîche, 252

Crepes, Smoked Salmon, with Cream Cheese, 115–17, *116*

Criterion Brasserie (London), 52

crostini:

Black Olive, Roasted Garlic Foam with, 213–15, *214*

Bresaola, with White Truffle Oil and Pecorino, 157

Kalamata Olive, Cod *Brandade* with, 122–23

cucumber(s):

Aspic, 250

Aspic, Soft-Shell Crabs with Marinated Cucumber and, 84–86, *85*

Juice with Pineapple Mint, 189

juicing, 184

"Linguine and Clams," Rick's, 162, *163*

Sorbet, Salad of, 226, *227*

Soup, Chilled, with Lemon Oil, 16–17

Cumin-Crusted Squab, Seared, with Huckleberry Gastrique, 154–56, *155*

Currants, Cold Foie Gras *Torchon*

with Peppered Pineapple Relish, Brioche and, 138–40, *139*

curry(ied):

Oil, 40

Three-Bean Salad, 39–40

custard:

Carrot Crème Brûlée with Blood Orange Reduction and Carrot Sprouts, 50–51

Roasted Shallot, 30–31

d

Danube (New York City), 126

Decker, Joe, 32

Divellec, Jacques, 81

Ducasse, Alain, 138

duck:

Stock, 242

Wonton, "Rick's Shooter" of, with Duck Consommé, 66–68, *67*

duck liver:

Cold Foie Gras *Torchon* with Peppered Pineapple Relish, Currants, and Brioche, 138–40, *139*

Mousse *Gougère,* 136–37

Warm Mini Foie Gras Club Sandwich, 146–48, *147*

e

egg(s):

Angel Hair and Artichoke Frittata, 58, *59*

Cinnamon French Toast with Turnips and Prunes, 75–77, *76*

Quail, Beef Tartare Spoon with, on Brioche, 179–81, *180*

Roasted Shallot Custard, 30–31

Emulsion, White Truffle, *46, 47*–48

English, Todd, 208

equipment, xvii

hard-to-find, sources for, 255

ISO canisters, 201

f

Fall Vegetables, Brunoise of, Braised Kholrabi with White Truffle Emulsion and, 45–48, *46*

Farfalle, Striped, Pasta Salad, 64, *65*

Fava Bean Soup, Chilled, with Seared Scallops, 10–12, *11*

Fearing, Dean, 72

fennel:

Caramelized, with Celery Root, 41

juicing, 184

Feta, Chickpea Spoon with Roasted Garlic and, 169–71, *170*

Fiddlehead Ferns and Radish, Salad of, 24–26, *25*

Figs (Boston), 208

Figs, Black Mission, Chilled and Grilled, with Mascarpone Foam and Prosciutto di Parma, 141–43, *142*

fish, sources for, 253–54

fish and seafood *amuse,* 79–127

Anchovy, White, Foam with Chives, 218

Anchovy, White, Yukon Gold Potato Chips with, 126–27

Beluga Caviar, Tower of Fingerling Potato with, 107

Caviar Staircase, 101–3, *102*

"Clams, Linguine and," Rick's, 162, *163*

Clams, Manila, Braised, with Sausage and White Beans, 124–25

Clams, Razor, with Charred Corn and Corn Puree, 81–83, *82*

RICK TRAMONTO is the executive chef/partner of Tru in Chicago. Tramonto was named one of *Food and Wine*'s Top Ten Best Chefs in the country in 1994 and was selected as one of America's Rising Star Chefs by Robert Mondavi in 1995. He has also been nominated four times for the James Beard Award for Best Chef in the Midwest, winning the award in 2002. Tru, which opened its doors in May 1999, was nominated for the 2000 James Beard Award for Best New Restaurant and named in the Top 50 Best Restaurants in the World by *Condé Nast Traveler*. Tramonto is the coauthor, with his partner Gale Gand, of *American Brasserie* and *Butter Sugar Flour Eggs*.

MARY GOODBODY is a nationally known food writer and editor who has worked on more than forty-five books. Her most recent credits include *Williams-Sonoma Kitchen Companion, The Garden Entertaining Cookbook,* and *Back to the Table*. She is the editor of the *IACP Food Forum Quarterly*, was the first editor in chief of *Cooks* magazine, and is a senior contributing editor for *Chocolatier* magazine and *Pastry Art & Design* magazine.

TIM TURNER is a nationally acclaimed food and tabletop photographer. He is a two-time James Beard Award winner for Best Food Photography, winning most recently in 2002. His previous projects include books in Charlie Trotter's series, *The Inn at Little Washington, Norman's New World Cuisine* (by Norman Van Aken), *Jacques Pepin's Kitchen,* and *American Brasserie*.

about the type

The text of this book was set in Filosofia. It was designed in 1996 by Zuzana Licko, who created it for digital typesetting as an interpretation of the sixteenth century typeface Bodoni. Filosofia, an example of Licko's unusual font designs, has classical proportions with a strong vertical feel, softened by rounded drop-like serifs. She has designed many typefaces and is the cofounder of *Emigré* magazine, where many of them first appeared. Born in Bratislava, Czechoslovakia, Licko came to the United States in 1968. She studied graphic communications at the University of California at Berkeley.